OF ALL THE LIVES
I'VE LIVED, THIS IS
MY FAVORITE

Dorothy,

Thank you for always believing in me. Together we can bring this book to life!

OF ALL THE LIVES I'VE LIVED, THIS IS MY FAVORITE

AN INSPIRATIONAL MEMOIR

LOTUS HALE HILL

NEW DEGREE PRESS

COPYRIGHT © 2022 LOTUS HALE HILL

All rights reserved.

Unless otherwise indicated, Bible verses are taken from the World English Bible (WEB) by Public Domain. The name "World English Bible" is trademarked.

OF ALL THE LIVES I'VE LIVED, THIS IS MY FAVORITE
An Inspirational Memoir

ISBN	979-8-88504-967-2	*Paperback*
	979-8-88504-968-9	*Kindle Ebook*
	979-8-88504-969-6	*Ebook*

To little Nicole, who trusted me enough to take her from that window, who fought the good fight. Now I can take over, and we can live and thrive together.

CONTENTS

AUTHOR'S NOTE	11
HOMECOMING: RETURN TO SELF AND COUNTRY	17
THE SANCTITY OF LIFE	41
THE INNER CHILD WHO STOOD BY THE WINDOW	49
BUT, I BELIEVE ME	61
MY LAST SUMMER IN THE HOOD	71
LIFE DEFINING DECISIONS	85
SHARED WOMB, SHARED WOUNDS	99
MAMA GOTTA HAVE A LIFE, TOO	115
GOD IS LOVE IS LOVE	129
TRIBE	139
MY SAFE WORD	151
ACKNOWLEDGMENTS	155
APPENDIX	159

To thine own self be true.
—POLONIUS OF WILLIAM SHAKESPEARE'S *HAMLET*

AUTHOR'S NOTE

I knew it was time to share my story when I came close to ending mine.

Like many privileged Americans, I had the luxury of remote work during the height of the global pandemic. On the heels of a national, racial uprising, an administration that didn't care whether I lived or died from gun violence or a virus that disproportionately affected Black Americans, shifting family dynamics that did not make space for the person I was evolving into, and general seasonal affective disorder (SAD), I had to get away.

Intuitively, I decided to spend three glorious months in Aruba, or, as many affectionately called it, Paradise. It was the first time I experienced American privilege. No one profiled me because of my Blackness, despite the ubiquitous nature of racism and anti-Blackness. However, at the end of my voyage, my attempt to return home to the United States painstakingly reminded me of the burden that comes with this skin. What should have been a seamless passport review through United States Customs and Border Patrol turned into an eight-hour inspection and two nights in a foreign jail (#FreeBrittneyGriner).

The first night, piercing screams and panic attacks were my only visitors. Suicidal ideation consumed my thoughts as the only viable option to take me out of my misery. However, once I snapped back into my body and logically considered the tools I had on hand—my shoelaces, the bars on the cage that held me captive, a six-foot concrete partition that separated the toilet from the metal bed—I realized actually going through with it would maim me more than get the job done. Finally, the adrenaline rush allowed me to quiet down and drift off to sleep. But just as the moon sets and makes way for the sun, a new dawn arrived. My angels marched in, and I was reminded that God's hand was and will always be a constant in my life.

I live to tell this story and share the wisdoms I've picked up along my life's journey over the past thirty-two years. These wisdoms are for those who wrestle with living beyond the box someone's cornered them in. It will resonate with those who wish to break free of the labels that hinder their full expression. It is for those who admire the courageous efforts of folks who live authentically and envision doing the same for themselves but have no place to start. It is for those who lead authentic lives that make them proud but long for the comforts of their tribe who will celebrate with them.

Here, I share what it means to be a pioneer of being the first in my tribe to accomplish major feats and do new things like going to college or believing myself when I remember I love women. I share how with courage and ingenuity, I ran for office in a city infested with patronage, corruption, and nepotism and earned the trust of people of all walks of life, spanning generational, racial, and ethnic identities. And at the eleventh hour, making the decision that this was not the life I wanted for myself and allowed the Universe to change the course of an election I thought I had already won.

I share how I have wrestled with the labels of being a daughter, friend, sister, Christian, and a woman and unearth parts of my identity I have knowingly hidden from myself for decades. I reveal the emotional scars from the consequential struggle of standing in my authentic self and facing hate and bigotry masked as seemingly principled opposition to who I was supposed to be, based on how I was born. Particularly for Black Americans, our given identities are at the heart of who we are and the lens through which we look at the world. This often comes laden with oppression and self-imposed limits that dictate who we think we can be and what we strive toward. We stay confined to the comforts of the familiar and daydream about what could have been. We quiet our deepest desires for more until they are rendered listless.

Upon these pages, I lay bare the perils of stepping out beyond predetermined limitations. I talk through the conscientious choice to no longer accommodate the comfort of dear loved ones if it meant sacrificing a life that brought me lasting satisfaction and pleasure and made me utterly content. A state of being that is a birthright to us all. In living this truth, I learned to hold space with deep compassion, knowing the tension I experienced reflected the insecurities and perceived shortcomings of those I called my own.

I grapple with who the church told me God was and reconcile it with who I experienced God to be during the darkest nights of my days and my greatest joys, reminding me that light exists, too. I share my journey of experiencing God's deep love for me in people that were said to be forbidden and not blessed. I grew in my understanding of what being in a relationship with God meant and how God is not offended by my questions, frustrations, or periods of estrangement. That once it's all said and done, there would be an outstretched, unchanging hand to welcome me back like the prodigal child.

Everyone has needs, but the reality of accepting that carries shame. I would hide what I needed from those near to me to save face and stay the strong friend, daughter, sister, and Black woman. But as life would have it, I would be placed in overwhelming circumstances that required me to use my voice, create and honor my boundaries to not only articulate the existence of my needs but specify how others should meet them. I vow to no longer betray myself and honor the highs and lows of life with tender kindness.

This journey is one of self-love—a concept that seems so lofty, enigmatic, intangible even, yet very clear on its purpose. I've found the first step in loving myself while in a relationship with others is not to neglect my relationship with myself and prioritize it above all other relationships. This can be difficult living in a preconditioned society of centering our life choices and identity around acceptance and the pleasure of other people that don't know what we're going through. This society asks us to contort our lifestyles, stifle our desires, self-gaslight, and not believe our own bodies when we know, can sense, and feel what our truth is. I want to make clear that this isn't a "me or them" zero-sum game, for we absolutely need each other to survive. However, we must individually and collectively strike a delicate balance to meet our own needs and enjoy relationships with those we lean on in our quest for survival.

The usual shame accompanying the need for love, shelter, security, and acceptance is a distant memory. Here, in my tribe, I don't have to hide my needs, nor do I worry I'm being bothersome if I ask for consolation or for someone to make space for me. I don't have to fear the rejection that seemed to keep me company more than the presence of a friend.

This moment of clarity is the fruit of experiencing some of life's most overwhelming experiences and accepting the truth that I can only do so much for myself. I must let others in to support me. It is up to me, up to us, to use our voices and say what we need, create and honor our boundaries that protect and affirm our human needs and how we need them met. With that same voice, we must make a personal vow to no longer betray ourselves and honor the highs and lows of life with tender kindness.

The journey of coming home to our most authentic selves is costly, and one many cannot afford because they assume roles required for mere survival. But if you can take risks for liberation, I encourage you to breathe life into the parts you've ignored. These are the parts you never let the world see. It's a cost that brings so much value in the end.

For me, this excavation has allowed me to make choices confidently, fully trusting my intuition. I can leave the light on for those who seek to know me intimately and love me deeply. I allow them to witness my unraveling and aid in my reassemble. This display of humanity is perfection and as good as it gets. Do understand, this journey does not happen overnight, and grace is imperative. Those that follow my story will learn the importance of listening and responding to their innermost knowings, be it a quiet whisper or a boisterous bellow from the depths of the soul. If anyone is to believe us and meet us where we are, we must first turn on the light and take the first look.

The price I've paid to clench my freedom doubles in value, and I marvel at the life I lead. My evolution has ushered me into a reality I could not have predicted. I fully receive love, quiet the nagging tugs that make me question my worthiness, and ignore the cyclical thoughts of losing it. My journey has compelled me to think expansively about family, embrace my chosen family, and take my rightful place in my tribe. Now, more than ever, I am surrounded by those who mean me nothing but good as we celebrate, advise, hold each other accountable, and mourn together. I take on life's challenges that attempt to rock me at my core and assess and proceed in equanimity. I hold on to God's unchanging hand when life's unpredictability pushes the limits of my sanity.

With this evolved perspective, I now look forward to continuing my journey, as the demands of life require more of me, being confident that there is order in every one of my steps.

HOMECOMING: RETURN TO SELF AND COUNTRY

"Squat five times and cough on the last one."

For the second time today, I experienced such an invasive search. Except for this time, the guards told me to remove my pants and underwear. They said it would come out if I had anything like drugs inside of me, so now was the time "to be honest." As if, up until this point, I had been lying.

The woman saw the look of fear and exhaustion in my eyes and muttered, "Sorry," under her breath. I wondered what she thought. "What's an American woman doing in jail?" Did she believe the stereotype that regardless of nationality, Black people were dangerous and indulged in criminal activity? Or were my insecurities getting the best of me, and she actually sympathized with me? I'm not certain.

Days before I was due to return home from Aruba, a progressive sense of overwhelming anxiety crept upon me. I went there for a *workcation* during the winter months of the pandemic in early 2021. Not only did my aunt live there, but Aruba is known as one of the safest Caribbean destinations for solo travel. Go, figure. When I left Chicago for my voyage of reprieve, some of my close familial relationships were quite tattered. I had ventured out of my family's house and made grand steps to exercise my independence by purchasing my first home. During the summer of 2020, I gave myself permission to love who I wanted to love, which unlocked a level of confidence and accountability to choose myself and make choices that were important to me, despite what anyone had to say. This level of self-ownership was new to my family dynamics. It unsettled the status quo and ruptured the foundation that formed my entire identity. I felt abandoned and left out because I outgrew the mold I shape-shifted to fit for so long.

The days leading up to my departure were rooted in the unknown of what awaited me back home. Though I was in the middle of a real estate transaction, there was speculation that financing would fall through. Furthermore, my family either couldn't or wouldn't give me the money I needed to close. Facing the potential reality of moving back in with my mommy did not sit well with me. Throughout my time in Paradise, I didn't speak much to my mommy or my sister, Jerrell. And in the beginning of my visit, I wondered why. I tried to maintain lines of communication, but it was never consistent, not even to this day. But I yielded. The space and distance allowed me to be fully present in my experience, rebuild who I needed to be for myself, and cultivate unwavering confidence to live my truth.

My time away allowed me to sit up close and personal with the parts of myself that could not move forward in my new phase of life and bid them adieu. My friend Ebony was the first person I told that I planned to take this trip. She said this experience would be good for me. Another friend, who was away in Mexico with her family, mentioned that a trip like this would change me, and it did in more ways than I could have imagined. When the thought of returning home consumed me, I realized I wasn't just anxious about what I was returning to. I was concerned about how I would hold on to the peace I found. The peace that was waiting for me once I pulled back the layers of fear, self-doubt, self-betrayal, people pleasing, and finally settled into the grace that God had been waiting for me all along. To transcend those fears, I embodied abundance, making way for the possible by surrendering to the Way Maker, releasing control of things that were indeed out of my *control*, and choosing to just *be*. This allowed me to be deeply rooted in knowing that all that is, is as it should be. This grounding would give me peace that transcends all understanding as I'd face the following days.

The morning I was to head to the airport, I was so heavy. I went to visit one of the first sites my aunt took me to when I first arrived in Paradise: Alto Vista Chapel. The Chapel is a popular tourist attraction many people of the Christian and Catholic faiths frequent to pray, meditate, and worship. Nearby stands the Peace Labyrinth, an intricate pattern of rocks that I believed was my own Garden of Gethsemane. In my final hours on the island, I spent time in prayer, walking along the rocks, asking God to lift the heavy burden that weighed my heart down.

I made it to the airport nearly three hours before my departure. However, despite this planning, it still wasn't enough time to breeze through customs. In a large hall full of mostly Americans traveling back home, customs only had one officer reviewing passports and one reviewing Global Entry. Sometimes I wonder if my fate would have turned out differently if I had Global Entry. As the hours passed, I barely moved an inch. Travelers all around me groaned and stressed about possibly missing their flights.

However, as multiple flight crews realized their planes were missing a significant number of passengers, they petitioned customs to move the process along. As I was already on edge, the fear of missing my flight made the ground beneath me crumble bit by bit. With each passing moment, gravel fell beneath me as I could see the bottom of this cliff. Finally, as I made it to the front of the line with nearly two hundred pounds of luggage, I could breathe a little easier and felt I was slowly retreating to solid ground. With fifteen minutes left to get to my gate, I flashed my passport, lowered my face mask, and pushed my cart through. Though I was apprehensive about returning home, home was the only place I wanted to be right now.

As I zipped around the corner, I physically met what my spirit had been wrestling with for the past few days.

"Hey! Come here!"

My stomach dropped, and I felt my body stumble off the cliff. Grasping for anything to pull myself up, I mustered every muscle to maintain my composure and fight the urge to physically crumble as I felt on the inside. I fell to my knees and burst into tears. I was just so close. The first and only time airport authorities stopped me was in college, and I actually missed that flight. But this was the United States Customs and Border Patrol under Homeland Security—a beast I had never known. Between being Black and the existence of the Patriot Act, when engaging with USCBP, I wasn't quite sure what my rights were. Knowing the harm police put one too many Black women and men through, I hopelessly obliged their demands.

His name was Rafael A. Flores, and he gives credence to that Word that says:

> The thief only comes to steal, kill, and destroy.
>
> —(JOHN 10:10, WORLD ENGLISH VERSION)

The officer commanded me to place my luggage on the conveyor belt for analysis through the baggage X-ray machine. My heart sank as I knew my window was closing to get to my gate. Tears fell from my eyes, and I pleaded to be able to go.

"Stop being a baby and be an adult. Just do what I say," he responded to me. More tears fell and more pleads. "Oh, now

I'm really going to search you." I couldn't win. No matter how compliant I was, it seemed Flores, rooted in hate and suspicion, was hellbent on causing me harm and would do so at all costs.

As the inspection went on, I saw the privacy and freedom that were my inalienable rights stripped from my hands, and I couldn't do anything about it. With my back literally against the wall, I slid down to the floor as tears flowed from my eyes. In the corner of my eye, I could see a White woman with a bag of fruit told to turn it over as her fruit was prohibited on the flight. "Oh, I didn't know. I had it for my family," she said without stopping, tossing the discarded food to the officer, along with his accusations. She and I clearly lived in two distinctly different worlds. As she turned the corner to rejoin her family, I noticed she stopped and took in the scene before her: all the contents of my luggage strewn across the metal inspection table and them telling me to stand up and stop crying. I knew I wasn't getting on that plane home. Near the cashier window, I noticed another White woman wiping tears from her eyes and closing her purse. Whatever she was guilty of, her payment of a fine allowed her to go free, although a bit shook up.

Rafael now had a sidekick to support the inspection. As the officers searched my bag, they hurled intermittent threats at me. Once the search concluded, anything that resembled drugs was taken into a closed-door room and tested for narcotics. Then the interrogation commenced.

Rafael emerged from a closed door and asked, "Do you know you have narcotics?"

"Narcotics!"

"Don't look so surprised."

"I'm serious. I don't know what you're talking about. I take those pills every day. I have a doctor's note on my computer."

He didn't offer me an opportunity to pull up the doctor's note. He ignored my response and continued with his conviction that I indeed was carrying drugs.

"You know you are putting my officers in danger with this stuff. You better be telling the truth."

> But when they deliver you up, don't be anxious how or what you will say, for it will be given you in that hour what you will say. For it is not you who speak, but the Spirit of your Father who speaks in you.
>
> —(MATTHEW 10:19–20, WORLD ENGLISH VERSION)

I knew nothing else but the truth. The pills he referred to were supplements I purchased between the United States and Aruba. I had notes from my primary care physician and my acupuncturist. I had a bottle of dandelion root that I purchased from a Peruvian vitamin store down the street from my house. I took these herbs to offset my chronic insomnia and the jaw pain from my temporomandibular joint (TMJ). Regardless of what was happening around me, I knew the truth was all I had. I didn't have the time or opportunity to try fabricating anything.

Nearby, another officer questioned a Caribbean Black woman who stood next to me. He asked her questions similar to my interrogation. He asked her how she had paid for her ticket. He told her he didn't believe she had saved her money. In an attempt to get a different answer from her, the officer mentioned she folded her cash the same way as her sister, who they had previously inspected. Nevertheless, she was free to go. With the courage I had left in me, I hoped that I, too, would be set free.

In between the direct questions, I snuck to text my friends to let them know I missed my plane. But I was explicitly told not to use my phone. Suspecting something unethical, when they weren't supervising me, I managed to turn on my voice memo recording to capture anything that could tell me what was going on in the room behind this ominously closed door. I noticed one of the officers saw me on my phone and told the inspecting officers. They emerged from the room, told me to hand over my phone, and write down my passcode. I obliged, willing to do anything to get free. When I received my phone two days later, I found not only did the officers stop the recording, but they deleted it.

Feeling defeated, I looked for hopeful faces and spotted a Black female officer. With tears in my eyes, I asked, "Can you help me?"

She looked at me as if she didn't want to get involved and responded, "I don't know what's going on!"

"Neither do I!" I retorted.

She poked her head into the office where the inspection was going on. She returned and said, "They'll be with you soon."

They finally returned. As tears of anxiety, mortification, and disbelief ceased to flow, I had settled back into my body and was able to answer thoughtfully and concisely, hoping this would appease the officers; that this was just one big inconvenience and I would soon be released. I was much more composed now than when I first arrived at the airport.

"When did you buy your ticket?"

"December first."

"How'd you pay for it?"

"I have a job."

"What do you do?"

"I'm a nonprofit fundraiser."

"When's the last time you worked?"

"Yesterday. I'm on paid time off because I'm traveling today."

To USCBP officers with integrity and experience, they should have sensed I wasn't a real criminal. But the ones that stood before me saw I had means, and they could extort me if I wanted my freedom bad enough.

I looked up at the wall and read the time: eight o'clock. For the last five hours, they accosted and questioned me. The officers told me to remove my jacket and take a picture, something like a mugshot. A picture that captured the fear, uncertainty, and anguish mounting deep inside that only my face could illustrate. I knew this picture would haunt me every time I tried to enter the country, bring undue suspicion, and always bring me back to this moment. I was sure it would be part of the country's database that monitored criminal movement and activity inside and outside the country. I was now one in the number.

Two female officers escorted me to a room for a body search. I complained about my foot hurting, and an officer noticed how it impacted my standing ability. I told her I didn't have my brace, and she asked me why I didn't have what I needed. I ignored her because I had difficulty accepting her empathy when her colleagues treated me so poorly. Throughout this entire situation, they treated me like a criminal, and now they just had to find the proof.

After the search, Flores ordered me to pack up all my things. I took a deep breath as I surveyed the table with all my things carelessly strewn on the table after the most invasive search I've experienced. Each item held a memory from the best time of my life, or so I thought: the stuffed animals I picked up for my nieces a few days before, the tarot cards I used during my morning rituals by the pool at my Airbnb, the top to one of the swimsuits that reminded me I had a beautiful body to be proud of. As I took my time stuffing my things back into my bag, I wondered how I'd look back at this trip and if these memories would still bring me joy. I wondered if I would still be proud of my decision to come here in the first place, or would I forever blame myself for getting into this situation. Maybe I should have let fear and trepidation win and stayed at home. I stuffed my questions along with my things and placed my suitcases on the cart to head to the office where Flores and his partner would prepare their report. Again, I asked if they could tell me what they were charging me with. Flores said I'd receive a receipt.

Sitting outside their office, I remembered I had a few more devices I could use to communicate with my family and friends back home. I pulled out my iPad as it wouldn't make any noise and drafted an email to give them a heads up:

Subject: **I feel I am being illegally detained**
US border pulled me out of line. Tested all my supplements.
Said it had
narcotics.
I missed my flight. I'm still here. Will keep you all posted.
I may need an attorney.
Don't call. They have my phone. I'm on my iPad.

No more than five minutes later, an officer came out of the office and asked for my iPad. I offered it over to him. I was down two devices and had two more left. I had to be more vigilant and careful. About an hour later, I saw the Black female officer from earlier. I asked if she could tell me what was going on. I was still unclear about why they were detaining me and what they were charging me with. She asked me if I had money. I thought of the twenty-dollar bill I had left from my ATM withdrawal and my credit cards I used over the last few months. She notified the officers that I had money and assured me I would be able to go home. Eventually, they drafted the report and brought me into the office. According to their *extensive lab analysis*, Rafael informed me I was carrying methamphetamines and ecstasy and that they were fining me five hundred dollars. I knew I had that in my savings and credit card and could easily pay that. He mentioned that if I couldn't pay five hundred dollars today, I would have thirty days to mail a check, or they would fine me five thousand dollars. I knew this was a farce but remembered to just stay in my body and stay focused on getting free.

When I asked if I could get a copy of the report for the third time, Flores said, "You'll get a receipt." He led me over to the cashier window, where I saw the older woman who had been crying earlier that day. I attempted to pay the fine, but the machine showed all three of my credit cards as declined. I thought that was weird as that's all I used during my time in Aruba, even at the airport. We went back to the office, where they reminded me I had thirty days to pay since I was unable to do so there. Now, clear as day, I noticed the clear plastic bag that held all the things they confiscated from me. I could see the word "Ecstasy" written in bright red letters on my American-made and sold facial wash bottle. At that moment it all became clear to me.

"Can I have your badge number?"

"No, I can't give that to you, but you can remember my name. Flores. There's only one of me here."

"Did they tell you it was going to be easy?" I became stone-faced with the realization I was in the middle of a shakedown, and they had no sympathy for my Black face. I wasn't going down the path he was tempting me toward.

"I understand."

"You understand what?"

"I understand."

I understood this wasn't about me carrying drugs. They knew I didn't have drugs. They wanted to extort me.

I stared blankly at him and didn't speak another word.

"Well, now you have to deal with the Aruban government."

I took a breath.

Rafael called the Aruban officers down, and they led me upstairs near the exit. I noticed everything was closed, and the last meal I ate was breakfast. Now, it was 9:00 p.m., nearing the COVID-19 protocol instituted curfew.

As I settled down and got out of the grasp of the American Customs officers, I hoped I could go home soon. I hoped the Aruban Customs officers would be as kind to me as the people had been my entire trip. At the end of the corner of the airport stood a Hyatt that I figured I could get a room at and get on the 11:00 a.m. Southwest flight back home. Home was the only place I wanted to be.

The officers instructed me to sit outside of the Aruban Customs office as the Aruban officer in charge took the bag of confiscated items and sat at a computer. I pulled out my computer and alerted my family that I was okay. A few young officers were working, and I overheard them talking about going to get food. I asked them if they could bring me whatever they got, and I gave them my last twenty-dollar bill and told them to keep the change. If there's one thing I learned, it is that American dollars move things. Back to my computer, I downloaded my family on what was happening again, assuming I'd be able to go home. Not too long after emailing my family, I got my food, but my body could only ingest a few bites of the burger and BBQ fries. I hoped this was an omen that freedom was near and I could head to bed soon. But after an hour of poring over the *evidence,* the lead Aruban officer told me they were going to arrest me.

Caught off guard and in awe, I asked why.

"It's a formality. The Americans started an investigation, and we must do so, too."

"But look at what they took. You know there's nothing there!"

He offered me a look of sympathy and resignation but knew his hands were tied.

I returned to my computer and notified my family that they were arresting me, and I didn't even know why. An hour later, two local male police officers came to take me into custody, threw cuffs around my wrists, and led me to a car. This was really happening.

The officers opened my door and commanded me to grab my luggage and walk into the police headquarters. I noticed all the familiar surroundings on the way here, then looked down at my wrist with handcuffs around them. This ride was different, and I felt it with every turn. Though I had spent three months here in Paradise, I hadn't gotten to every nook and cranny on the island. However, this was an out-of-sight area I never thought I'd see.

The officers watched me struggle with my luggage, struggling for control with the cuffs. I assumed this to be part of my punishment as a drug trafficking Black woman. I tried to focus on responding to my reality rather than reacting.

I walked into the police station and left my luggage at the door. After they booked me, a female officer walked me into a closed room so she could search me. This time, I had to remove all my clothes. Afterward, they escorted me to the back of the jail, where they housed the inmates. It was dark. A stench of human waste hung as heavy as the humidity in the air, making it difficult to breathe. I couldn't believe this was my reality. I had to escape, but I couldn't, and that's when I left my body. From that moment until I left the jail, I experienced the next two days hovering above my body, observing the world as if it were a museum, not connecting with any of it to save the sanity I had left.

Without a pillow or blanket, the officer led me to a cell with a 2' x 6' metal-covered concrete bed, two tall blocks made from the same material. One block concealed the toilet, and the other block hid where I would stand to shower, a wide-open pipe that flushed water down so I could clean myself. Levers that only the wardens could access controlled the water and toilet.

Finally, I made it to my cell to be left alone with my thoughts. I was now in the belly of the beast. It was the worst night I've ever survived. From screaming fits to panic attacks, I pleaded for my release, but no one came. Eventually, an officer came. Through his broken English, he asked me if I was having a panic attack. He encouraged me to breathe and offered me cold water.

When was I gonna get out? The thought drove me mad. Though many things have been out of my control, at least I could move. But this moment was nearly more than what I could bear. I fancied the idea of climbing on top of one of those blocks and falling headfirst. I also thought about taking my shoelaces, tying one end to the bars and the other around my neck. But logic would remind me I would maim myself more than take myself out. It wouldn't be until the next day that the officers remembered they should have taken my shoelaces before they locked me away. I never got those shoelaces back. But it's not like I could wear those shoes again anyway.

Still unaware of what they arrested me for and what my charges were, I finally drifted off to sleep. By the morning, I called for a guard and asked when I could speak with someone. They said 9:00 a.m. Having been exposed to the sun for so long, I understood the time based on where the sun shined. And around 9:30 a.m., I asked if I could speak with someone. Finally, a few minutes later, they told me to come up front as the consulate would be calling.

The angels had come!

Back in the same room as my strip search from the previous night, a woman greeted me as the court-appointed attorney but was there to notify me that my family had already retained an attorney on my behalf. Then two detectives walked in and handed me my passport and United States Department of State documents to fill out. They said these would give the consulate the right to communicate my whereabouts and status to designated people.

Moments later, the consulate called. He was in nearby Curaçao and gave me the rundown of my rights, which weren't many. According to Dutch law, as Aruba is a former Dutch colony, a person held in jail cannot receive phone calls from anyone other than the consulate and their attorney. I could expect to have a trial within three days. If the prosecutor has reason to continue an investigation, they could detain me in jail for up to ten days. If the investigation continues, they will transfer me to prison, where I'll get more amenities, his words not mine, like soap, a pillow, and blankets, and can speak with my family. When he said ten days and prison, I dropped to my knees. When I looked up, an older gentleman entered the room and wrote on his clipboard, "Ebony Lucas called me."

The angels had indeed come!

I met with my attorney in the interrogation room in the back. He was quite skeptical of me at first. After hearing about the case, word had gotten around that I was the American trafficking ecstasy. He asked me where I stayed on the island, and he mentioned he knew my Airbnb hosts. I thought about my conversations and paint and sips with my host on random Saturday nights and hoped they'd say good things about me if he asked them about me. He asked why I had so many pills and I answered, rather self-consciously, defending my choice to care for my body holistically. He could see the wearies hanging from my eyelids and could only assume I had a rough night. I didn't have to tell him it wasn't a good night. He asked if I needed to go to the doctor and if I was desperate. I told him I was. He assured me he'd come back and visit me that evening.

When I returned to my cell, I had food waiting for me. It smelled really good, and I would have eaten it, but I couldn't eat, and was severely constipated. I attempted to shower, hoping fresh water would perk me up. As I was wiping myself with my hands—I had no soap or sponge—armed guards appeared out of nowhere and came to escort me to the hospital. During my visit with my attorney, I told him I was desperate and needed to see a doctor. Between my ailing mental state, constipation, and sleep deprivation, I needed help. I had never been more excited to go to the hospital, anything to get out of that cell. God ensured I didn't have to spend more time than what was required locked up. God knew too much alone time would not be good for me.

So I quickly threw on my same filthy clothes. The officers tightened handcuffs around my wrists and escorted me to an armored car. Every part of this experience blew me. Me, in an armored car, with handcuffs, tightened around my wrists. I was no more than one hundred twenty-five pounds and under five feet tall. But I guess they couldn't take any chances.

I knew the direction of the hospital, and I could peer out of a small window at my once familiar, now estranged surroundings as the armored truck made its way to the place I got my COVID test from the day before. It's amazing how one event can instantly change your perception.

Two guards handled me. The female officer seemed to take well to me. We talked about her experience of living and working here. And I told her about my experience. A few Dutch doctors saw me, and a particular female psychiatrist seemed to empathize with me. I told her what was happening. I shared that I couldn't sleep, was constipated, and thought about hurting myself. She told me she'd get me something to calm me down and help me go to sleep and use the bathroom. She encouraged me to pray and be patient.

Despite my circumstance, I was in awe of how God's presence was made apparent through all the people I interacted with. This allowed me to be still and feel safe, being confident that I was not alone. Once I received my prescription, we headed back to the jail and I back to my cell. I felt lighter, and I had a peace that calmed me.

Not long after returning, my attorney arrived to visit me. I later learned that though he anticipated I'd spend another night in jail, giving me a visit was something I could look forward to.

Chris, my attorney, shared words from my sister. "She wants you to be strong for her because she's being strong for you. She's burning lots and lots of candles for you."

That made me smile because I knew she'd keep those candles burning until I came home. He asked to take a picture of me to send to Ebony. I fashioned a halfway smile, but the story was in my eyes.

"Maybe try some yoga. Or meditate. Try to get your mind off things."

Chris informed me that contrary to the American way, according to Aruban culture, if you ask to speak to an attorney before the police, you've got something to hide. So when given the opportunity to tell your story, tell the truth, regardless if an attorney was present or not.

As I returned to my cell and sat down, I told myself I would be in this present moment. That I wouldn't concern myself about when I would get out. I just needed to get through the next moment, then the next, then the next. I wondered why this happened to me, and I thought about all that I had seen. I always wanted to make sense of things, and I wondered if I would one day uncover corruption in the United States Customs and Border Patrol department. Would I bring justice to the many Black women unjustly accused and detained across the Caribbean? What did God want me to see that I could help amplify? What difference could I make after surviving this disaster? Whatever it was, I knew God would reveal it to me over time. I just had to get through this moment.

Once I got back into my body, I took Chris's advice and moved my body. I did a few sun salutations and breathing exercises. Then my spirit started singing, and the praises came up my throat and out of my mouth. I remembered my ancestors sang while in bondage. I now understood how they could still cultivate joy, create beautiful things, and maintain a will to live, despite enduring enslavement.

"It's going to be a good Friday!" Spirit confirmed for me.

I chanted this. It was a mantra. Tomorrow was, in fact, Good Friday. I knew it would be good for me, and I would be getting out.

Before I drifted off to sleep, the warden finally informed me of the charges they were holding me on. She prefaced it with the fact that I wouldn't understand it because the writing was in Dutch. I folded up that paper and tucked it into my shoe. Today, I display it on my refrigerator as a reminder of God's grace and provision.

"We're off today. We only came to work for you."

Those were the words the two officers I briefly met the day before said to me.

"We stopped by here yesterday, but you weren't here. So, we had to come back today."

I just knew they were all about sick of my American ass at this point. Between my sister's calls to the jail and consulate, my aunt's visits to the jail to drop off toiletries that I didn't get until it was time to leave, and the periodic check-ins about my state of being, they were ready to get me out of there. I still do not know the full extent of what went on to get me free. But ain't that just like God's protection and provision?

Finally, after forty-eight hours, I was able to share my story. While giving my testimony to the officers, I learned that the Aruban authorities tested eighty percent of what they confiscated, which was all negative, refuting what the Americans accused me of possessing. Once they submitted my story to the prosecutor, one of the officers made a call, and he said, "Okay, let's go. We're taking you to the airport."

I asked if I could use the bathroom up front, and they said, "Yes, you're no longer a prisoner."

A reminder that my freedom was beyond my grasp for the past few days.

I walked into the main office where they booked me two nights before and reunited with my belongings. Behind the desk, the warden who handed me my charges the day before read the report with my testimony. "Incredible!" She couldn't believe how wrong the American officers were.

I told her and the rest of her staff that the American government hates Black people, especially Black women. I shared that I felt safer here than I did at home. Why do you think

I'm here during a pandemic and not there? They were dumbfounded and couldn't believe that a country like America would do this to their own people.

We immediately left the jail, loaded my luggage into the car, and headed toward the airport, toward freedom. Once we arrived, the officers carried my luggage to the door and wished me well. I stepped out of the car and immediately called my mom and my sister to let them know I was safe and heading home. I had no trouble with Southwest to switch my expired ticket to the next flight home. Thankfully, an auntie was on the other side of customer service, and I shared a synopsis of my story. She sympathized with me as she had a niece about my age who, too, loved to travel. I felt so covered and so wrapped in love and care.

As I entered the airport, the freedom I saw yanked from me had found its way back to my embrace, descending from heaven by way of my angels that came to my rescue. When I boarded my plane, I sent a text to my aunt to let her know I was safe and on the plane.

"Freedom is fragile," she claimed.

I had never thought about freedom before that day. It was just something I had, something I didn't have to fight for or negotiate. When they confined me to that cage, I had to ask for the toilet to be flushed, for the water to run so I could shower, and even the exact time of day. These questions weren't simply about being courteous but rather about asking for permission to participate in simple tasks I take for granted.

As I boarded the plane, heading home, I knew life would never be the same. However, I knew I had the freedom to choose to live a life that made me proud. I could choose who I wanted around me, who I wanted to love, who I called family and friends, whose approval I would seek, and choose who would be my hero. It would always be me.

THE SANCTITY OF LIFE

When a baby is first born, their very presence shifts the energy in any room. This new life commands so much attention: from the volume at which people speak to the support needed to hold up their heads. When expectant parents get word of new life, they offer up praises to the Creator. It renews their enthusiasm, and a gust of life returns. As the baby takes its first breath, deep gratitude is felt, and a new journey begins with the rise and fall of its chest.

This life is sacred. The breath affirms life in the body. The breath, I have found, reminds me that despite what's going on around me or in the world, as long as I have breath, I can enjoy the gift of life. It keeps continual praise on my lips. The gift that grounds me in the moment and gets me back to my true purpose, which is to breathe and to be.

I didn't always think this.

In fact, I remember a time when living didn't seem like enough reason to stick around. The muck and mire of the world's most dreadful and hateful parts had mounted on me. As I surrendered to the pressure, letting darkness win, and adopting a bleak forecast for my future, I got further away from the gift of grace each new morning offers. When I spent two nights in jail in Aruba after a failed attempt to return home after a three-month voyage of reprieve, I considered three distinct ways of hurting myself. And funny enough, the jail warden told me the next morning to hand over my shoelaces. The basis of my decision to leave this life was my lack of control and my belief that I didn't have any other option. My present reality was like nothing I had ever seen, and I wanted, needed out. They wrongfully accused me, and their accusation wasn't even clear. I didn't have the opportunity to defend myself. All power and sovereignty I mustered over the past three months seemed to dissipate as each minute passed. However, the consolation and words of encouragement from my attorney reminded me of the tools I had to revive myself, and one of them was my breath.

Once I returned to my cell, I took in deep breaths, ignoring the stench from the exposed toilet and pipes. I moved my body to allow the breath to flow through me. Every breath revived the parts of me that the weight of the world's muck and mire gripped tightly. I reminded myself to get through the next moment. I had to breathe and be in that moment, not worry about how much longer I'd be there. It was the breath that grounded and encouraged me to keep seeking the next moment, and the next, and the next.

Once I settled back home, the impact and reality of my detainment settled into me. Flashes of various events rushed in: the bars that closed in my cell, the scent of rotting bodily fluids, the heated back and forth I had between one of the jail guards, and the overall feeling of disempowerment of not knowing my rights as the United States Customs and Border Patrol officers surveyed every inch of my belongings. I now had a new life, a new home, and a new awareness of the world. They ripped away the naivete of the old that once gave me comfort, and those images haunted me and caught up with me. So much so that one day I tried to physically outrun them. On Memorial Day 2021, I had plans to meet up with my family for a picnic. I didn't feel up to socializing, but I knew I shouldn't be alone.

Earlier that day, I envisioned my body strewn across the back of my one-year-old leased Honda Accord in my deeded parking spot below—visible for all my neighbors to see. I tried to imagine how my vigilant and boisterous downstairs neighbor would react. I thought about the call my mommy would receive once they could get in touch with her. I knew that though I wouldn't be sad, my mom would be. I didn't want my last thought to be that for the remainder of her life, my mommy would live with the dark cloud of my choice to leave hanging over her. My mommy's heartbreak kept me from doing it. In this instance, as in many throughout my life, I vacillated between calling my mommy's response a parachute that I pulled on or taking care of her emotional needs. Either way, my mommy was my parachute and kept me grounded.

I kept those thoughts to myself, hiding them from my plain sight, and they resurfaced about a month later during a therapy session. Before my episode, I wanted to see a new therapist. I felt my old one didn't prioritize me the way I needed. Because I showed that I was self-sufficient and didn't come off as one of her more pressed patients, she didn't give me the support I knew I needed. However, once I shared my Aruba ordeal with my community, my friend, who is a therapist, suggested I look into the eye movement desensitization reprocessing (EMDR) treatment, as it helps integrate traumatic incidents.

Once I shared my suicidal thoughts with my therapist, I cried because I realized how far I had gone, and ending it all seemed to be the most logical option. I cried even more because I almost forgot about it, put it out of my mind, and even passed it off as an insignificant bad day. Was it dissociation or a case of the *strong Black woman* where I assumed the feelings of despair and the thoughts were normal? As I revisited it, I confessed to my therapist, "I really did think about killing myself a few weeks ago... Wait, did I actually say that out loud?" I couldn't believe the words left my mouth. A blanket of sadness swaddled me as I felt for that girl who lived that reality. As she tried to outrun the thoughts, I watched her drive around the city, not knowing where to go. And though she could join her family, that wasn't where she wanted to go. Snapping back into the body, I remember feeling so lost in a city that I could navigate with a blindfold. I felt so disconnected from reality. All I could share with my sister was that I couldn't make it because it was a hard day.

Making my way through my dark cloud has been a difficult but worthy journey. Since working with my new therapist, I have made progressive strides in managing my reality and the present moment. Whenever my once constant companion of hopelessness comes to visit, I make space for it, sit with it, and then show it to the door. When the feeling of listlessness creeps up, I no longer look at it as normal and continue with business as usual, attempting to stuff it away. Instead, I take it as an opportunity to listen to it and see what I experienced, or what part of me needs attention, or that I need some rest and intentional self-care.

As part of the sacredness of life, I've found the gift of God's love in human form. I realize I have a tribe willing to stand with me and see me through my dark clouds. My tribe affirms my reasons to live because they wish to see me transcend these moments, and if they see value in my life, I can too.

I came that they may have life and have it abundantly.

—(JOHN 10:10, WORLD ENGLISH VERSION)

One member of my tribe, Sista Shamon, holds weekly morning grounding meditations. During our moments of astral projection and visioning rituals, she always reminds us to breathe. It is always good to hold on to the breath to navigate the encounters with our shadow selves and integrate those truths that contrast with the light. The sacredness of the breath affords us the sweet opportunity to care for ourselves the way no one else can. To be the balm for those wounds that the shadow self carries. To embrace the shadow self, rather than outrun what we can never detach from. I once felt burdened to be the one responsible for showing up for myself. However, I learned it is a privilege to give such attention to myself, and it informs the kind of love and care I wish to receive from others. Just as I am going through and navigating unknown terrain, so is every other person around me. And while we can aid, support, and witness each other along our respective journeys of life, we can hold space for each other to tinker with meeting our own needs.

Tapping into my breath allows me to exercise agency in how I respond to the moment, be it a moment of joy or a moment of sorrow. Tapping into the breath confirms that though I don't have control over the world around me, I can control how I perceive it. In this way, I can choose what kind of experience I'll have as this life is mine to live, a gift to be opened every moment of every day. Tapping into life offers the discretion to choose the lens through which I observe and engage in the world. I can be as active or apart from the world's ways as I wish. Tapping into life unearths the sovereignty vested within me, allowing me to choose freedom or bondage. I can decide whether this is my heaven or my hell.

Ultimately, I've learned life is to be lived, and it's not enough to simply be alive. Living is an active form of gratitude that gives honor to the sanctity of being alive. I've found that being alive, though the bodily faculties are operating, is absent of the invigorating thrill of choosing and walking tall in my God given sovereignty. But when I choose to live, love, be present, and allow the breath to revitalize and sustain me, I breathe in creative ways to enhance my daily walk.

I wish that as long as I have breath, I revel in the living. At this juncture, I have worked to upend myself from what others told me I should do and how I should live my life. Now I live in a way that existed only in my dreams and inspired by my soul's compulsion to seek it out with all my heart. It is a life that grounds and reminds me even in my darkest moments, there is more to this life than this moment. Yet and still, this moment, though heavy, needs to be lived.

Breathing meditation
I invite you to do this breathing exercise as you make your way through my stories.
Inhale.
Exhale.
With each successive breath, relax the muscles in the jaw, the shoulders
and lumber by lumber, loosen the grip around the spine
inhale
exhale
unclenching the backside
let air flow through the lungs, down to the stomach, into the intestines, and relax
allowing the nutrients to absorb, satisfying hunger
keeping the gaze low, imagine sending the breath to the temples located on each side of the head
Envision that every breath allows the blood to flow easily through the veins, losing the tension around the head
inhale
exhale
inhale
exhale

THE INNER CHILD WHO STOOD BY THE WINDOW

I can see myself standing in the living room, peering out the window. I'm squinting my eyes. The sun is out, and I hope it's shining for me. I hope its rays guide my father from wherever he is to my house so he can make good on his promise of coming to see me. Seconds spill into minutes, pouring into hours, and finally, I drop my head in resignation. Once again, he's not coming. My mommy, checking in periodically, has no words of encouragement because she's also heartbroken by another empty promise.

Dating and romantic relationships would almost always trigger me to step back in that moment. I'd have a great date and then get ghosted for a few days. I'd end up back in my mommy's living room, back looking out of that window, feeling that angst and abandonment well up in my chest. In seconds, I am a little girl, looking, anticipating her father's love, hoping to unlock it within the right man, but it would never arrive. I wanted answers as to why this always happened. Why did my father think this was okay? Would it be different next time? Was I not a good enough girl? I was left with silence and a crushed spirit to make up the answers. I must not be worthy. My idea of love must be different from what love actually is. As I already am, I am not good enough to be loved, so I must do more and be more.

I have tattooed the scene in my mind. I'm the victim now, and it's everyone else's fault, sinking deeper into the story I've told myself since I was that hurt little girl. That is until the day I came back to my younger self. And this time, instead of watching from afar, I stood next to the little girl inside of me. I called out to her. I asked the little girl inside if she wanted to go somewhere else, finally giving her an opportunity to use the voice that the silence from her estranged father took from her.

As a child, my father never apologized or brought up his absence. It was one of those "what's understood don't need to be explained" situations. My father's silence taught me not only did I not have a choice in the matter, but I had to accept it. I was not empowered to use my voice, nor was I given the space to articulate how it broke my heart. The silence and abandonment my father offered told me that this is what I should expect in future relationships. Whenever he finally turned back up, I was to accept him with open arms, no questions asked.

Back in that living room, I eventually walked my little self away from the window, but it was a process. When I first started visiting my younger self, I was always greeted with a stoic view of the back of my head. Each time I visited her, I asked and waited, offering myself the space and time to make up my mind. Each time, I'd come back to greet me until, finally, one day, I turned toward my older self and contemplated taking my hand and stepping away from the window.

For most of my life, my father and I were estranged. He was an infrequent presence in my life from birth to about third grade. But after that, my memories get fuzzy, and I don't remember him much until high school graduation. I was in first grade when my grandma Hill, my father's mom, made her transition. I was devastated and cried in my mommy's arms when she broke the news to me. My father lived in Grandma Hill's house, and she was always a delight to visit. Now that she was gone, what would my visits with my dad be like, if they continued at all? Though I cried because she was gone, my spirit must have known I was mourning the loss of the tattered relationship my father and I had.

I didn't go to the funeral. Even when I did interact with my father, I was offered no choice in anything. My naps were mandated, and I had to drink milk. Trivial things but important to my little self. I wanted no part of spending another moment with him. For a short time, I regretted not attending that funeral. However, I realized funerals are for the living, and my Grandma Hill is and will always be with me.

With my grandma's passing, the accountability that held my relationship with my father together had dissipated. From the moment I made it earthside, my Grandma Hill made it a point that he would honor his commitment and see about his child. However, once she was no longer here, he had no incentive to maintain a relationship with me. There was a blur from third grade when he took me shopping for summer clothes and then high school graduation. Somehow, he learned that it was graduation. He called me the day before and said he would be there. I left him tickets at my Granna's house, but he never picked them up. As an attempt to make up for it, when I made it to college, he said he didn't want me to work and promised to take care of me. That money never came, and by my senior year, I had three jobs and made almost $30,000 as a college student. Now that I know more about who my father was then, I know he really would have liked to make good on his promises. But the hurt, pain, and self-numbing he succumbed to would not allow the man I know today to stand up tall.

Most interactions with my father were very negative and hostile. He is a very intense person, strong and forceful. He's always been a no-nonsense kind of guy. But I now know at a very young age, he built up a wall to protect the little boy inside, the one who lost his innocence at a very young age. I picked up on this even through our estrangement. As a child, I didn't know he experienced extreme state alteration, so I rarely interacted with the real man inside. His representative, whom I had come to know as my father, was callous and arrogant. He shirked from his responsibility and often deflected when the light fell upon his transgressions. As I got older, I used the voice I had and all the courage I could muster to bring up how he hurt me and never supported me. I mentioned how my mommy always took care of me, and his response was to remind me of the time when she didn't want me.

"You know she wanted to abort you. Asked me for the money and everything," he said.

"Well, look at me now. She took care of me, regardless." I retorted.

I buried that deep inside. I knew the news of my birth called my mommy to consider all options. At the time, my father was dating another woman when he met my mommy, so she was never his main. She knew his inconsistencies wouldn't translate to being a stable father. Moreover, she may or may not have still been married to my sister's father, so legally, who my father is up to the courts. Just kidding, my daddy claims me. She even considered allowing my Granna's long-time friend and customer to adopt me. She and her husband were middle-aged and had the home and income to care for a new child.

My father's vindictive responses often showed he knew his actions weren't acceptable. He knew he had caused harm. He was unable to address his internal turmoil, and his options were to numb and exist in an altered state. This didn't allow him to make space for me, accept responsibility for his actions, or even admit he caused me a great deal of pain.

As my golden thirty-first birthday approached, my father and I reconnected. As an adult, this was our usual cadence: reconnect, talk, hang out, he'd ghost me, then when he came back around, I'd bring up his absence, and he'd say, "you still on that?" I'd then get upset, be triggered, and put up my wall. My wall gave the little girl inside the protection she wished she had when she stood at that window, waiting for him to come. With no tools to scale, he'd light dynamite or drive a bulldozer to get to the other side, hurling insults at me through pages of inappropriate text messages and calls in the middle of the night. He disregarded my requests for him to stop. In turn, I'd block him for six months to a year.

Rinse. Repeat.

This went on from about 2015 until 2021. This time, I had reached near my limit, not optimistic that it would be different.

He planned to send me money for my birthday. He called the night before and asked if I had plans. It's my birthday, of course, I did. My father didn't always have consistent employment, as he was a painter and workman. He said he might have a job tomorrow and couldn't confirm plans to hang out, though he wanted to. In an instant, I was back at that window waiting for him to come. It was up to me to protect myself from making that my reality, and I was not waiting around for him, especially not on my birthday.

"I can't hold a space for you 'just in case' you become available."

My boundary somehow offended him.

"Yeah, okay."

We ended the call.

On the morning of my birthday, I woke up immensely heavy. My tears greeted me. My first call came from my college roommate. We always FaceTime on our birthdays. She was in Texas at the time, awaiting notification of her dental residency placement. In the video, her son was crawling all over her, and I got to meet him and catch slobbery virtual kisses. Here I was, in my apartment, in my new bed I just bought on my Macy's credit card, and I was crying on my birthday. We spent almost two hours catching up, and our only interruptions were from the baby and random comments from her partner lying on the other side of the bed.

She shared with them who I was and what I had been up to. She rattled off my most recent accomplishments of running for office and being friends with an international hood legend Chicago rap star. Hearing her speak of me in the way she did was comforting because I caught a glimpse of how I wished I could see myself. Bogging myself down with who I was trying to be and not giving credence to who I already was. Striving, never being. For my birthday, I planned to host a full moon fire pit sister circle with some friends later that evening, but the way I was feeling, I leaned toward canceling. My roomie encouraged me to keep my plans. I hung up the phone and started to get ready for the day.

In my adult years, my father became a man of his word. He did end up sending the money via Zelle but felt he was entitled to my time. So he called nonstop, as he often does when he doesn't get a response or when he feels I'm intentionally ignoring him. At the time, I was with a friend and couldn't answer. Once I called him back, he was irate. As if he bought some counterfeit tickets from Craigslist and they duped him into sending the money before receiving them. Don't ask me how I know what it feels like. The conversation was quick, and I thanked him for the birthday gift. He was still upset we couldn't see each other, I guess, assuming he should get some face time for his contribution. We ended the conversation, and I went on with my day.

The next day, I tried calling him but got no response. I imagined a terrifying turn of events happening after not being able to get in touch with him for over a day. I questioned whether not making myself available for him sent him over the edge. I didn't know what he was capable of doing. Finally, I decided to call my big sister, Regan, my dad's longtime girlfriend's daughter. I asked Regan if she or her mom had heard or seen him. She responded dryly, "He is probably somewhere mad." Then she continued on, "Ya know, Lotus, you really don't know your father. But I'll tell you, whatever your mom did, it was the right decision to keep him away from you." I was off that day, so I had time.

For the next two hours, my sister walked me through what it was like to live with my father. When he and my mommy met, he was in a long-term relationship with another woman, Regan's mom.

"I was so excited when I learned I'd be getting a new little sister. But once you were born, and I realized you weren't coming around, I knew something wasn't right."

As she rattled off her experiences, I paralleled my experiences of where I was in life. When the holidays rolled around, she realized he was with them and not with me, his baby girl.

"What kind of man wouldn't be with his own daughter on the holidays?"

She recounted his volatile personality and moods. She even expressed concerns over his mental health and borderline personality disturbances. He was rarely romantic with her mom, often showing up empty-handed to holiday functions, never a gift giver, and if he did, they were cheap.

As my sister went through what it was like growing up with my father in the home, I gave her the space she needed.

"I experienced such mental abuse and turmoil, and so did my mom," she lamented. "I'd wonder why my mom would keep coming back to him. He never contributed to the house. We almost lost the house. My grandmother had to leave Los Angeles and move back in with us so we could keep the house."

She took a breath.

"But it wasn't always bad. He was like a father to me and is a grandfather to my son. He taught me how to drive."

That was the most honest conversation I had with her and about my dad. More truth telling was to come.

It's February 2021. I'm standing in my studio Airbnb in Oranjestad, Aruba. It had been four months since I last spoke to my father. My cousin, who looked to my dad as a second father, called me and told me he had just admitted my father to rehab. This wasn't the first time I got word he was heading to rehab. But this time, I had a voice and could navigate this experience.

"What kind of substances does my father use?" When my father was in rehab before, he wrote me a few letters while he was away, but I didn't get around to writing back.

"Heron (heroine), coke, and alcohol."

"Oh," was all I could muster.

Sometime during the previous summer, this same cousin called me, telling me I should reach out to my father because he was going through a rough patch, and hearing from me may give him some solace. Without even thinking about what that could mean for me, I obliged, disregarding the recommendations my therapist offered and the emotional boundaries I set to protect myself. Like clockwork, it continued the nasty cycle that was our relationship. But now, in Paradise, my new environment gave me the space to think and the courage to say the hard things. The truth was, I couldn't go through that again. I wouldn't. And if I had something to say about it, which I did, I always did, it wouldn't happen.

After taking a deep breath and remembering my own agency and that I have a choice in who could access me, even my own father, I said, "Last summer, you called me, encouraging me to reach out to him. And it didn't end well. I can't be there for him the way you're suggesting because it turns out the same way, and I get hurt. And I can't keep letting him hurt me."

My cousin understood and respected my stance.

"I do want a relationship with my dad, though," I reflected.

"You will. One day," he reassured me.

At that moment, the young girl standing by the window turned, looked up at me, and smiled. With her hand in mine, we walked away from the window and toward the sun. To change how I reacted to triggers, I had to change how I responded to them, and that was the only thing within my control. I realized I had to take responsibility for my actions and honor the boundaries I put in place to keep me safe and set a new cycle in motion. I couldn't control how my father treated me, but I could act in such a way that protected me. I am my own hero. No one will save me but myself. To get to that moment it took time, patience, consistent action in the moment, and hope that things would indeed get better.

Whether or not I believed it, it did get better. Once my father completed treatment and was in active recovery, we reconnected. On that June day, we grabbed fried shrimp and walked along the lakefront. On that day, I met my father. The guy who was no longer numb. The man who stood up and told the other guy, the altered guy, to stand down. On that day, I met my father for the first time.

BUT, I BELIEVE ME

My Granna has been working since the age of twelve. She's now eighty-three, a licensed cosmetologist, and keeps a client on the books now and then. She doesn't need to work as my granddad has a decent pension and "is a good man" and provides for his family. However, my Granna's conviction that she must work so she can have her own is a symptom of poverty that never quite went away, even after she's aged into life as gracefully as she has.

My Granna was born in Birmingham, Alabama, and is the eldest of four girls. Together with her mommy, Mama Gussie, her grandmother Big Mama, and her sisters, they traversed from the Deep South to the North during the second wave of the Great Migration with 4.3 million Black Americans (Gregory 2009). Our roots took hold in Chicago as they traveled from Newark, New Jersey, and Cleveland, Ohio. Mama Gussie had an incentive to settle in Chicago as her older sister, Aunt Catherine, settled there as well.

Early on, my Granna knew her family was poor. She retells a poignant story of living in an apartment where each family had one room. The six of them piled into one room with a stove. A couple with no children lived in a nearby room. The woman would make food and offer it to Granna and the family. At the time, Black folks only made so much money, and with six mouths to feed, those dollars could only stretch so far. Not having enough triggered Mama Gussie, and she demanded the girls refuse the food despite the need. With hollow bellies and the growl of hunger pangs, my family's legacy of refusing one's personal needs for pride and ego began.

"Oh, thank you, but we're fine."

At that moment, my Granna learned what to do with needs she couldn't meet. Mama Gussie, a woman who, somewhere along the way, learned to mask her hurt and shirk perceived judgment because it was shameful not to have the capacity to deliver. So, as it would go, she admonished the girls, forcing their hand to refuse something they so desperately needed—food. With tears in her eyes, my Granna would oblige, though bewildered as to why they couldn't eat when food was within arm's reach and hunger ravaged their hollow bellies. Shame and the deafening silence of their harsh reality were what the bare cupboards and lint-filled coin purses could offer them. Did Mama Gussie feel judged? Would her neighbors assume she was an unfit mother if she accepted the food? Was there a larger lesson she wanted to teach her girls? The world didn't sympathize with Black people, especially unwed mothers with a different father for every child. She didn't want her girls to think someone would hand them the world on a silver platter. They had to learn to work and earn to ensure they had everything they needed to survive.

Those words, "we're fine," stung my Granna's six-year-old impressionable heart, leaving an indelible imprint. The truth was, they weren't fine, but they couldn't let anyone else know that. This set the course of how my Granna, her sisters, and future generations would respond to their needs. The impact would be insidious and would manifest as beliefs of unworthiness, scarcity mindsets, fear of and inability to ask for what you need, and equating productivity to value.

The magnetic force of a scarcity mindset, a by-product of poverty, paralyzes the mind in a thought pattern that arrests the imagination making the case that more is possible. Then there's the shadow of shame that hovers above unmet basic human needs. My Granna carried shame with her need. She learned early on that not only was being needy prohibited, but if you could not meet your needs, no one else could, which must mean you're unworthy to accept. And if you're unworthy to accept, you certainly couldn't ask. If she couldn't accept help from others, she had to make it for herself.

According to Urban Dictionary, to hustle is to strive headstrong and voraciously toward a goal (Stixx 2019). And then there's a picture of my Granna. She's about twelve years old and decided she would no longer be without. It was left up to her to change her reality. Hustlers are smart. They observe and make sense of the world, understand the systems, and leverage them to create the world they want. As a child, my Granna understood money could change the world, and getting a job was the best way to cash. She tells this story of when she was barely twelve years old, she got a job at a factory. She couldn't work a full day because, despite confidently offering an age-appropriate date of birth, the receptionist knew better. To my Granna's chagrin, the receptionist, a perceptive sympathetic woman, knew my Granna was underage and painstakingly told her she couldn't work there or they'd be violating child labor laws.

Why was a twelve-year-old going to such lengths to work? My answer is poverty. At the time, the United States' involvement in World War II brought more economic opportunities to ameliorate the impact of the Great Depression. However, circumstances for Black Americans were still meager. Black families earned one-third the income of White families, and Black Americans were twice as likely to be unemployed than White Americans (Jeffries 1996). In short, my Granna grew up poor, and she felt it. It was all she could see.

My Granna's hustle made it so I didn't know I was poor until I was an adult. But Mama Gussie's lessons were still deeply ingrained in me. These lessons influenced how I approached getting my needs met and my confidence to ask others to help me. On the one hand, I inherited Granna's ambition and relentless will to work hard and hustle. A sniper-like focus and commitment to the grind would come in handy when I persevered to accomplish major feats, like writing this book or running for political office. On the other hand, shame and silence passed down like family heirlooms would rationalize trivializing a genuine need for fear of judgment and the belief that if I hadn't worked for it, I was unworthy and undeserving. For much of my life, in little and small ways, I would treat my needs like a newborn baby learning to self-soothe, with no loving parent coming to coddle them.

But eventually, it would come to a head as the weight of the global pandemic pressed down on my shoulders.

For the first three months of the pandemic, I kept up most of my usual schedule: seven to nine hours of uninterrupted sleep, working out three to four times a week, eating good meals, journaling and reflecting, and biweekly therapy appointments. Though I missed the regular human connection, I loved having fewer distractions so I could stay balanced and make sure I had what I needed. A once busy calendar, filled with after-work happy hours and God knows what, made way for quiet evenings and undisturbed time to think and sit with the reality of the moment we were all collectively thrust into.

As the seasons changed, so did many of my relationships and identity. Earlier that summer, I fell in love with a woman for the first time, and it ended as the leaves on the trees changed colors and fell to the ground. As I evolved into this new person, some familial relationships that were part of my foundation started to shift. They could no longer accommodate who I was evolving into. This new version of self remembered a part of me that I forgot about long ago. A part that gave me the passion and fullness of a love connection I had never experienced with men. My newness showed up in old relationships where I once quietly obliged but now would use my voice to articulate my needs. Who I once was and the people who defined me deteriorated before my eyes. This change also manifested physically as the block I called home for over twenty-five years fell to great peril. For the first time, I questioned my physical safety. So finally, six months into the pandemic, the weight of "these unprecedented times" fell on me.

I became a recluse and fell into an all too familiar feeling of hopelessness cloaked in depression. Depression isn't new to me, but this was the first time I actually acknowledged it and how it impacted my work. Beyond genetic predisposition, the need to work connects to an ancestral struggle rooted in slavery. Seeing my Granna care for her family the way she did and motivated by a resolve to never meet poverty again, I never saw her stop to care for herself. The result: fibroids and diabetes. If she stopped to care for herself, the money flow would slow. But even beyond that, who would she be if she stopped working, even momentarily? After all, it had been her focus since she was a kid. In turn, who would I be without work? Work said that if I did well enough, I was worthy. Up to that point, I maintained my family legacy of ignoring deep-seated needs, despite losing a grip on reality and happiness.

As I watched the proverbial candle burn at both ends and the brunt of burnout loomed, I looked around and reached for a lifeline. I remembered a good girlfriend of mine had recently left a toxic work environment after taking a formal medical leave from work. To my understanding, the Family Medical Leave Act (FMLA) was for new parents and folks recovering from a major medical procedure. They were medical conditions you could see with your eyes, not ones you had to prove. But what's more proof than how I felt? Up to that point, I didn't believe what I felt. It was in my bloodline to quietly ignore whatever came from inside, begging for immediate attention. However, the quiet moments given to me by the pandemic allowed me to hear and feel what was coming up intimately, and I could no longer ignore it. I entered a relationship with those hurts and gave them the credence they so deeply deserved.

I had to own the parts of me that hurt, the parts that were weak. Carrying shame cost me peace of mind and my voice. Giving those parts the say they needed allowed me to accept and integrate them. In doing so, I relinquished the stronghold shame had on me, disrupting the cycle that haunted my foremothers. A true dismantling of generational curses. The fear of being judged as unproductive or not worthy dissipated as I affirmed that my humanity warranted me rest and said I was worthy of it. I didn't have to work for it.

Once I settled my need within myself, I had to settle it against my identity as a worker. While I found the courage to give voice to the parts of me that ached, so much of my identity intertwined with who I was at work and how I produced. While the voice I offered to myself allowed me to develop deep inner compassion, I had yet to explore what this meant for me as a person. Work meant I was valuable, and up to that point, I believed I needed to work to earn my rest. My generational legacy told me that what I could produce was who I was. It was intoxicating. Up to that point, I continued to chase opportunities, titles, and responsibilities till I was exhausted. But it was all fleeting. I never fully felt satisfied because of those things outside of myself. Returning my voice and believing me when I said it hurt ignited the enduring, most liberating process of detaching my value from the roles I had. I learned how to take them off when it came to matters of caring for myself.

Finally, I could articulate my needs to my supervisors to explore the best course of action. Still grappling with this newness, I wondered how long I needed. I crafted multiple scenarios in my head, including the holidays and personal time off. Then the intoxicating desire to be needed and important crept up my spine: what if I took half time off? "That would defeat the purpose," Ebony reminded me as I laid out the multiple scenarios. "What you don't want to happen is you come back in January not as rested or confident as a full-time break would provide," she reasoned. I swallowed the angst, knowing it was a tug of the familiar self-neglect, and stepped into the embodiment of care and utter concern for my well-being.

To my surprise, my supervisor and leadership were beyond supportive of me taking the full time off. They truly embody one of our organizational core values of *we care for each other*. After getting the paperwork completed by my primary care physician, I started closing out projects and notifying collaborative team members that I would be taking time away. With each successive step, I took toward providing for my needs, the parts that once ached inside of me calmed and began to settle. And then the healing occurred.

This experience has been the genesis of a new way of being. It allows me to take breaks when I need them, monitor how I'm feeling, and make necessary adjustments. I've learned there's no reward in suffering, and exhaustion does not equate to genius or productivity. The hustle that was once a disjointed staccato rhythm that solely focused on the parts of me the world could see, the parts that were once dependent on external validation and value-based productivity, makes way for a melodic crescendo that allows me to embrace all parts of me previously hindered by shame and ache, and apply the balm of self-compassion and be rooted in worthiness.

In these conversations with self, I forgave myself for the neglect and self-disregard. My atonement would be accountability and believing the hurt and need the *first time*. Today, I am entitled to choices and freedoms that poverty stole from my foremothers. I can create a new legacy where walking in sovereignty and meeting one's needs is a right and the default.

MY LAST SUMMER IN THE HOOD

—

> *Weathering: They pull out one piece at a time, and another piece and another piece, until you sort of collapse. [...] I thought that Jenga metaphor was very apt because you start losing pieces of your health and well-being, but you still try to go on as long as you can.*
> —DR. ARLINE GERONIMUS (DEMBY 2018)

When I decided to run for office, one of the first things I knew I had to do was to raise money. I reached out to anyone I met, no matter how long since we last spoke. One person, in particular, was a woman I went to elementary school with. We grew up in the same Englewood neighborhood, just ten blocks apart. In recent years, we connected via social media and began following each other's exploration of adulting. When the time came, I asked her if she could sit on my campaign launch host committee. She ecstatically agreed to it and sent me affirmations and kudos throughout the campaign. After the campaign launch, I reviewed my donors to mail thank you cards. In doing so, I noted my former schoolmate, a Spelman graduate and attorney in the State's Attorney's Office, moved to one of Chicago's most affluent neighborhoods. Curious to learn more, I reached out to her and asked her when she made the move. Her response, "Oh, girl. Last summer was my last summer in the hood in Englewood."

The 1990s were dark and difficult years that left an indelible scar on the Chicago neighborhood I called home. In 1992, federal agents, in concert with local law enforcement agencies, executed "Operation Englewood." Agents seized businesses, homes, vehicles, and aircraft and made several arrests to stem the supply of crack cocaine to Englewood dealers (Recktenwald 1992).

In 1995, Chicago, no stranger to national news, made it to the *New York Times* (Terry 1995). A serial killer roamed the streets of Englewood, leaving the remains of ten strangled women, disposed of like trash, littered throughout gangways and alleys.

In July of that same year, the city suffered from mercurial high temperatures, claiming the lives of 739 people during the devastating 1995 Chicago heat wave (Te 2021). Blacks Chicagoans, those in poorly ventilated homes and the elderly, were among the most affected. The Englewood neighborhood, a victim of racial segregation, poor social infrastructure, and residents that didn't trust or know their neighbors, was the hardest hit. It would take decades for this neighborliness and community trust to grow.

These tumultuous times were also unkind to my family. In that same year of 1995, my mommy at the wheel, me in the front seat, both of us without a seatbelt, and my older sister in the rear, made head-on contact with a car that did not observe the right of way, and it drastically altered the course of our lives, and our car totaled. But by the grace of God, we were left generally intact, despite an imprint of my mommy's skull on the cracked windshield, me with a busted lip from hitting the glove compartment, and my sister with a minor scratch on her neck from her seatbelt. This accident made our world stand still and suspended our movement and options.

We had to move from one of my Granna's buildings in Dolton, a south Chicago suburb, and into her home where my mommy grew up, in Washington Heights, a well-to-do Black neighborhood post-White flight, to recuperate. I am acutely aware that God's protection and provision and the utility of my Granna's diligence and perseverance shielded us from experiencing homelessness. She provided for us beyond a safe and warm place to lay our heads. Neither my father nor my sister's father were in the picture. Thus, my Granna was an additional contributor, sometimes the only, to support our family during our formative years. Together, my mommy and Granna provided all our physical needs and most of our wants. Funny enough, I didn't know I grew up poor until I became an adult. For me, this childlike purview nurtured my innocence and cultivated an optimistic disposition toward life and ambition to surmount life's challenges.

By early 1997, a little over a year in my Granna's home, my family moved to an Englewood Greystone that my Granna bought with my grandfather's death benefits in the 1980s. At the time, I was heading into the second half of first grade and attended a magnet school. Magnet schools were the few public schools that offered school busing in the city. This is where I learned that I had to leave my neighborhood for better opportunities and experience a life my environment was incapable of offering.

Mommy worked various types of jobs. From serving as a call operator at the Regional Transit Authority (RTA) to leveraging her entrepreneurial chops and gift of gab to sell cosmetics like Mary Kay. As a child, I remember glancing at my mommy's paystubs, and though I had little context for how much money was enough, $816.21 seemed like a lot to me. However, as an adult, I understood differently, and all I can say is God bless single mothers.

My mommy never let us go hungry and always found a way. She was very enterprising in ensuring provision showed up. Hence, we never missed out on getting our basic needs met. We went to good schools, we had appropriate clothes for when the seasons changed, and we celebrated the holidays. Though I qualified for free lunch, if I wanted Subway for lunch on days I went on field trips, she would make sure I had it. But, when we moved to Englewood, it seemed our environment reflected the reality of our financial situation.

Although we lived in Englewood, our mother suspended our outside playtime until we went to Granna's house. That's where our bikes were stored and where my childhood friends lived. My sister and I didn't play outside. It wasn't explicitly said that we couldn't. It just seemed to be understood, given our new stomping grounds.

The first intimation that my new community was among the least desirable was when it came to my friends coming over for a sleepover. I had an elementary school friend whose parents adamantly refused to let her spend the night. And in the eight years of our friendship, she only came over once and that was for a few hours. I never took that as a slight at me, but my mommy understood it intimately. Despite these affronts, mommy never dissuaded nor forbade me from staying with my friends. Yet she carried the scorn from my friend's parents, who thought their child was too good to come to my home.

As I matured, I continued the course of leaving the community for opportunities. I attended one of the jewels of Chicago Public Schools, Whitney M. Young Magnet High School, where Forever First Lady Michelle Obama (Class of 1981) graduated nearly twenty-five years before my matriculation. It was here when it became palpable that there was something different about how I grew up, and my childlike naivete could no longer ignore it. At Whitney Young, I came to understand the difference between the economic classes. My friends grew up middle-class, living in communities like Beverly, Kenwood, and Hyde Park. My classmates were the children of the elite: elected officials, civil rights leaders, business executives, and hall of fame athletes dubbed the greatest of all time. This was a public school, by the way. Many leaders who possessed highly sought-after board positions, led city agencies, or were popular entertainers, were Whitney Young graduates.

It was through my friendships with the Black elite that not only did my perception of class difference become keener, but it became evident in our lived experiences. One of my best friends, Brianna, grew up in Beverly. Both of her older sisters were Whitney Young graduates and went on to study at Howard University. I recall during one conversation we had during sophomore year, she shared that her family was going to spend a week in Arizona. For the life of me, I didn't understand why they would be going to Arizona *just because*. It did not occur to me that people go on family vacations. To my recollection, my family only reserved time outside of Chicago for funerals and family reunions, and the latter had become less common as our elders passed on. The concept of a family vacation blew my mind.

I was also a first-generation college student, and while college was a viable option for me, my family conversations never emphasized it as my next step. But in recollection, perhaps they just assumed that was where I would head. Nonetheless, my high school impressed this next step within the minds of every student, and the question wasn't "Are you going to college?", but rather "Where are you going to college?" My schools, located outside of my neighborhood, cultivated my exploration of life after high school and a pathway that no one in my family had ever traversed. Though my mommy and sister had a few college semesters under their belt, they had yet to complete it. It would not be until I completed my first year of college that my mommy reenrolled and earned her bachelor's degree. We both graduated with our master's degrees in 2016! She attributes me as her motivation to return.

It wasn't until my junior year of high school that I understood the implications of having Englewood resources as your only option versus the privilege I had to explore more of what made a *good life*. As a graduation requirement, Chicago Public School high school students must complete forty hours of community service learning. I opted to volunteer as a tutor and homework aide at the community center that stood a block from my home. I never participated in events or programs and barely stepped foot in the building, but I felt called to complete the bulk of my hours there. During one after-school session, I remember working with a middle school student. He experienced significant challenges in completing his assignment because he struggled to read and comprehend. I remember being able to read fluently in first grade and was even tested for the gifted program. My school had tracked me among college-bound students who could command more difficult studies.

Here was a child who lived a block or so away from me, and because I possessed a round-trip ticket to the best Chicago had to offer, our options for a future were strikingly different. Mine, one with strokes of a vibrant vision, colored with varying hues of promise and hope, and his, a bleak outlook, color gradients mimicked gray clouds and made it difficult to see one foot in front of the other. Our academic experiences and our readiness for the world would determine how successful we could be and whether we could have a more prosperous future than the generations before us. For me, I would be more educated than anyone in my immediate family, and my salary one year out of college would best my mommy's most successful year, and an appetite to consume all the world had to offer. For him, more of the same and meager glimpses of what more could look like were made visible through social media and the city's more affluent neighborhoods. It would be this experience that accented my pursuit of public service.

While my community has a dreaded history of violence that continues to this day, I never questioned my safety. Unfortunately, in Chicago, like other most populous urban cities across the country, the violence usually roams on certain blocks, almost always in poor Black neighborhoods; thus, the exact location where you reside will influence your experience. In fact, a former classmate of mine, famed basketball player and Chicago hometown hero, Derrick Rose, shared a distressing account about what it was like for him to grow up in Englewood in a single-parent home. He lamented having post-traumatic stress disorder and feared for his safety anytime he heard loud noises in or around his home. He admitted he could not discern between jovial roughhousing and imminent danger (Pierce 2021).

For the twenty-five years I lived on my block, I heard the stories, read the news, and watched how people's eyes got wide like saucers when I told them I lived in Englewood. In fact, when one of my college friends was in town and saw where I lived, based on what he thought of me and how I presented on campus, he was surprised I lived in the hood. Never judge a book by its cover. And just because someone is a victim of systemic racism, historical divestment, and redlining doesn't mean they have no sense or are any less human than you. Nonetheless, I never witnessed the violence, and rarely would an incident occur near my front doorstep. But that changed at a glacial yet consistent pace over the last few years.

It was my last holiday break in college. I planned to participate in the Michigan in Washington Program during my final semester. I interned at one of the nation's leading progressive policy think tanks. I'd live within walking distance from the White House and Dupont Circle. It would be the second time I experienced DC. The summer after my sophomore year of college, I interned in Senator Durbin's office in the Senate Hart building. That summer, Congress passed the Reinvestment Act to restore the country after the 2008 recession and extended unemployment benefits that kept my mommy and sister afloat. I had burgeoning political aspirations then, and that experience helped me to narrow my focus to local pursuits.

My educational experiences laid out a grand scheme for me to imagine a future beyond what my surroundings showed me. One foot in both worlds inspired me to not only explore what my future could look like but how I could build bridges between the two. I wouldn't call it survivor's guilt because I never questioned why I was the *lucky one* to *get out*. Still, it was more so a moral obligation to right systemic wrongs that made me an exception to the unfortunate destiny in store for those from my zip code. This was a very tall order for one person to commit to. And over the years, the way I contributed to this cause evolved.

About a week before my departure to DC, I decided to take a walk to the local corner store. I craved what I call a *hood delicacy*: flamin' hots with nacho cheese. Don't judge. You weren't there! You can take the girl out the hood, but you can't take the hood out the girl.

At the time, I was dog sitting for my uncle, and Posie the Schnauzer was due for a stroll. As I prepared to walk out the door, my mommy sparked up a conversation that delayed me for a bit. Finally, I headed toward the store, and in true millennial fashion, I walked with my head down, distracted by my social media timeline. Shots rang out as I made it a half block from the store. I looked up and saw a man walk from a car on the corner, busting shots as he walked toward a Church's Chicken. The shooting left four people wounded and two dead. I turned around and ran home, not sure what direction the gunman, who returned to his car, was heading. And to this day, I know it was God speaking through my mommy who held me up, or I otherwise would have been caught in the crossfire.

Since then, that corner has been a bastion separating two gang factions. And in subsequent years, it has brought more bullets and instilled mounting fear among those who call 65th and Green Street home.

I was never ashamed of my community nor tried to hide where I lived. Showing up in the rooms and spaces I was afforded access to, I became poised in translating the raw experiences of my community to an audience that had influence and power vested in their net worth, which was often pronounced by the color of their skin. Where I came from informed my outlook on life and the purpose driven work I was called to do. In many ways, I believed the work I did here on Earth would play an integral role in improving the quality of life for Black folks in Chicago. Based on my limited experiences, I believed public service was the best way to affect the change I believed we needed.

My 2019 run for public office was a grand effort to really show up for my community. But a sobering loss cracked me open and allowed me to make an inquiry into who I was becoming and to find a balance between how I showed up in the community and how I could show up for myself.

The need to leave my community for basic commodities was nearing its expiration. I found myself spending more time shopping for quality produce and healthier food options outside of my community than what local gas stations and mini-marts offered. Resources I frequented, like ATMs, would most often be out of order or understocked in my community versus those in more affluent neighborhoods. And I could no longer ignore the vacant lots, dilapidated buildings, poorly cared for lawns, and litter-filled streets. The consistent surveillance and whirring of helicopters every night kept me tossing and turning.

I found myself driving to the north side for acupuncture every week during the summer of 2021. The office, located in the Ravenswood/Lincoln Square neighborhood, was home to former Mayor Rahm Emanuel. The well-manicured lawns, the diverse food offerings, and the general sentiment that people felt safe, enamored me. That same summer, my block had experienced weekly shootings for seven consecutive weeks. One of the last shootings that cemented my inclination to leave forced my sixty-something-year-old uncle to the ground at 6:30 a.m. as he checked the mailbox. A car full of kids let loose warning shots in the air, attempting to instill a lethal retaliatory warning to their opposing targets.

I searched for homes to purchase but limited my search to local neighborhoods I was familiar with. There is a saying that Chicago residents, often like New Yorkers, rarely venture far from their homes. However, after that summer, I expanded my search and decided it was time to make a transition. Finally, in April 2021, I closed on my first property in a welcoming South Shore condominium.

With my move, I surmised that I would be no good to my community if I felt as lost and as devastated as those I wanted to help. Additionally, I began exploring more of my identity as someone who had good ideas and a caring heart. I was a person who deserved more, and I would not be heralded as a martyr whether I stayed in the community or transitioned out.

My ultimate goal has always been to build a bridge so my community could experience and create a life for themselves beyond the crumbling vestiges of a once thriving Black community. And to be clear, this does not mean to integrate or assimilate into a White dominant culture that has never been tolerant of the rich diversity of Blackness. The truth was that whenever anyone has been assigned a place in life and offered no tools to define themselves on their own terms or envision life as a human, regardless of the color of their skin, they confirm those limiting beliefs and reflect it in their behavior. That's what was going on in my hood. My people did what they saw. They lived how they were treated. White Supremacy's mission accomplished. The consequences of slavery sending shocks through the veins of Black Americans centuries later.

Now, almost a year in my new home, the new perspective has allowed me to excavate more parts of who I am and what I like. I am more committed to seeking environments that honor and cultivate peace. In years past, I sought a life in the corrupt ridden Chicago political landscape. I had a narrow view of how I could show up and contribute to my community. Clothed in the savior cloak that many talented *strong* Black women don, I once found solace in being needed. With this cloak comes an implicit resignation to a life of struggle and a monolithic Black experience. But as Beyoncé once said, it is our birthright to live, and how we choose to do that is up to us (Knowles-Carter 2019).

I gave myself permission to live a life of ease.

LIFE DEFINING DECISIONS

It was two days before Election Day, and I was beyond autopilot. The human mortal version of myself tapped out long ago, and I knew that God had given me all the strength I needed to get to this day. My mom and I packed into her Mini Cooper, with yard signs and 4' X 4' signs strapped down in the back. Sitting in my lap was the Spanish translated campaign literature I planned to hand out to potential voters in the Back of the Yards neighborhood as they left Sunday Mass. My ward spanned so many neighborhoods on Chicago's South Side: from the historic Woodlawn, through parts of disenfranchised Englewood—my stomping grounds—to the city's lowest voter turnout neighborhood of Back of the Yards, home to many undocumented residents.

I made it to the runoff in my quest to become the Alderperson of Chicago's Twentieth Ward. From a field of nine, I came out in the top two during the primary election. Now, it came down to me and a union-backed organizer, who outspent me three to one. But I was determined, and no one would outwork me. I made the decision to run almost three years before Election Day. And through those three years, I busted my butt to earn the respect of my constituents of all backgrounds: homeowners, renters, seniors, middle school students. My face and name were everywhere, and though I didn't win, I made a lasting impression that earned the respect and chagrin of politicos and other influential people across the landscape.

I remember the moment I made the choice to run. It was a Friday night, and ABC 7 news covered the story of the Twentieth Ward incumbent's federal corruption indictment. He was the third consecutive alderman to be indicted and ultimately convicted on federal charges. I truly believed my community deserved better, so much so that it became my campaign slogan (#WeDeserveBetter). I wholeheartedly believed it and exemplified this truth in the way I ran my campaign and the vision I set for how I would govern.

As we made our way to the church, I sank into the front seat. At a red light, my mom asked, "Do you really want this?"

I sat with that question, searching for the answer. Up until that point, social and local media dragged me, saying I was a plant, representing big corporate interests. Critics and opponents couldn't believe that I was running a completely independent campaign; money flowed through my hands like sand as I leveraged my networks to raise over $120,000. I didn't get many endorsements, but when I did, they came from Grammy Award-winning artists that promoted my candidacy on their social media, and affectionately referred to Beyoncé as Auntie Yonce. It was unheard of for a young Black woman from the hood to make this type of progress, especially rivaling nationally renowned Chicago unions. Running in Chicago is no easy feat. As Abner Mikva, a former Illinois US Congressman, federal judge, and Democratic presidential adviser, once said, "We don't want nobody that nobody sent." Meaning, you have to wait your turn, or the efforts of an insurgent candidate, like me, would be futile.

I was unrelenting in my pursuit to build a political organization that rivaled eight competitors, some twice my age, and I kept big union bosses on their toes and sweating. I reached voters that lived in homes for decades and at no point had a candidate or elected official knock on their door. My specific neighborhood was gerrymandered in such a way that candidates vying for the coveted aldermanic seat never needed to knock on the doors from my hood. Thus, I was intentional in placing my campaign headquarters in the heart of Englewood: 55th and Halsted. This won me a lot of loyalty support. One day, as I stood outside of the early voting polling place, a woman hopped out of her car with the literature that my team left on her door. She walked up to me and said, "I'm voting for you because of this." And she pointed to my office's address. My people felt seen; my campaign shined a light on their plight that had long been swept under the rug, kept them in the dark just as inaccessible broadband internet disconnected us from the ever-expanding world.

I was running because I really gave a shit. I grew up in the hood, but I was not of the hood. The baggage and trauma that comes along with growing up along the darkest margins of society, I only knew tangentially because that's where I laid my head. It was because of my proximity to affluence and opportunity that protected me from the harshest blows and realities of the cruel world. Instead of hopelessness, I nurtured ambition and self-confidence that not only did I matter, but when I saw something, I could do something about it. Growing up with middle-class friends revealed to me that the environment I grew up in did not have to be this way. Considering I had an unlimited round-trip ticket between both worlds, I could position myself to construct a bridge to expand greater access to opportunities for my community. And I believed that running for office would afford me that. I wanted to put an end to the abuse.

As I tried to answer my mommy's question, I pondered the opposition I experienced. I had hella haters, and they were not afraid to show it. At one point, my runoff opponent sent out text polls to gauge support, and when my supporters selected me as their desired candidate, the poll continued to lambast me with false accusations about my character and qualifications. My friends would send me screenshots of the polls, completely surprised that they would say such a thing. I witnessed how my name was dragged through the mud, and even still, I pressed on. That was what I was signing up for, right? And so, when my mommy asked me the question of whether I really wanted *this*, not only did I have to agree to become an elected official and lead, I also had to accept that I would have to wear Teflon armor every single day to protect myself against the attacks lodged against me, either by the media or the people I chose to serve. In attempting to answer the question, I faced the reality of my potential future and whether I really wanted this for myself.

Searching for context, I thought of Kim Foxx, the Cook County State's Attorney. At the time, she was in an embroiled challenge about her choice not to pursue charges against a celebrity attention-seeking case that went wrong. No one died, simply a tarnished image tinted by embarrassment. I thought about Foxx and how, despite her experience, she continued to serve the people and implement the changes she promised during her campaign.

"Well, somehow Kim Foxx does it, so I can, too." It was the best answer I could offer.

In two days, I would wake up for my final Election Day. Up until that day, I felt like I was going to win. However, mommy's question gave me space to acknowledge the reality of a win and actually settle into what I was doing, take my foot off the gas and turn off the cruise control. Her question spoke to a part of me that had nearly dozed off at the wheel. As I stared down the barrel of the gun that would determine my future, I realized that I didn't want this for myself. The truth was, I felt horrible on the inside and outside. I hated seeing distasteful crude things said about me, and I had to add more armor to keep going. It made me cringe that people hated me so much that they tore up my signs every chance they got. Though I thought it protected me, the ironclad armor I wore also hardened me, made me cold, sometimes despondent. I didn't feel good and didn't want to do something that didn't make me feel good.

As I thought about what it would mean to lose my election, I wondered what other people would think of me. I worked so hard to get where I was today, that if I lost, what would people think of me then? I noticed that when I put myself out there and walked in bold confidence, it always held up a mirror to onlookers who lacked confidence and belief in themselves. Their response to me was almost always to tear me down to the image they really saw of themselves. I had experienced that time and time again, and I had enough. It felt horrible because I wasn't in touch with what I actually thought of myself. I accepted the reflection on how others perceived me. I didn't realize that when they saw me, they saw what they thought they couldn't be. In turn, I didn't acknowledge the fully loaded boss bitch competition I brought to the table. I worked so hard to be someone I already was but couldn't see it. How sad.

From the very beginning, others told me the other guy would win. The other guy was an opponent who ran in the previous election and then became the ward committeeman. He thought he had it in the bag. The coveted committeeman seat, though unpaid, was an opportunity to drive voter turnout, influence voter preference, and gain visibility for pursuers of paid elected, more powerful offices. From the very beginning, seasoned politicos and anyone with a general interest in elected politics doubted my ability to raise money. And once I raised the money, I later learned that there was speculation that I wouldn't know how to build a formidable team and devise a plan for victory.

I could assume I'd get resistance from outsiders. That was par for the course. However, I didn't expect to get so much of it from the woman I loved the most: my mommy.

When I first told my mommy about my decision to run, she didn't meet me with the grandest gesture of support. In fact, it was as if she was deterring me from pursuing something I felt deeply called to do. At one point in her life, my mommy, like many Black women, had dreams, but as she aged, faced disappointments, and made missteps, the compounding effects dragged her down and discouraged her from trying many things. Over time, she became less and less risk averse to protect herself from disappointment. Never fully having anyone in her corner that believed in her, despite what they had seen or believed was possible for a young Black girl. With time, I understood this to be my mommy's truth and how it triggered her when I dared to dream bigger than I could ever imagine. Nevertheless, as I showed her what was possible through discipline, commitment, and risk-taking, she eventually caught on and ended up being my number one cheerleader. Notwithstanding the truth, her initial discouragement was hard to adjust to and weighed on me as I stepped out into the beginning of my journey. Thereafter, the vigor to *prove* myself was deep-seated.

As I answered, "Do you want this," I had to take the good with the bad. Indeed, I wanted to serve my community and represent them in a way they truly deserved, in a way that honored their humanity and made them feel seen in places where others held concentrated influence and power. However, it didn't sit well with me that it would be at my expense. I didn't want to be a martyr, and frankly, no one should ever have to be one to make a difference. I was young, not even thirty, and had my entire life ahead of me. Making this choice so early in my life would leave an indelible imprint on me that would change me forever. I quietly made my decision that this was, in fact, not something I wanted in my life. The universe would acknowledge it and make it so in a resounding agreement two days later.

On Tuesday, I woke up and faced the day as I had planned. Being confident that I had given this thing all I had, I was proud. They say that the only thing that's worse than a failure is the regret of not trying. And not only did I try, I gave it everything I had. By 4:00 a.m., I was up and waiting for my campaign adviser to pick me up. There was a different feeling in the air than on previous Election Days. We quietly drove to my office, where I met my poll watchers, volunteers, and campaign staff. Before the polls opened at 5:00 a.m., I made sure to start our day in prayer. Thanking each and every person that showed up. I was there because of them.

I had a packed schedule to hit every precinct and every polling place at least once. Visibility is key in these races. However, as the day grew on, I sensed that change from the mountain top experience from the weekend. The energy shifted the moment I truthfully answered mommy's questions. At each polling place, my Senior Adviser checked the poll numbers and kept referring to the low voter numbers. He had been around the block a couple of times, and as a seasoned candidate, he knew that for a noninstitutional candidate like me, low voter turnout was not in my favor. Though it was the last day, my last shot, I cried for a nap. And I was given one hour to rest for lunch. That's how over it I was.

At 7:00 p.m., the polls closed, and I headed home to wash away the day. As I sat on the phone with a high school buddy in my robe, I watched the results roll in. "Damn, G. I think I just lost my race." I hung up the phone and started getting an influx of text messages. "How are you doing in the polls?" I didn't bother to respond, annoyed by a question Google could answer. Even though I acknowledged I didn't want a win, the icky place I was in was still uncomfortable. Tired and irritable, all I wanted was more sleep. A loss is a loss, despite not wanting to win. And losing sucks. As I reflect, I realize I was so hurt I didn't have the words to know how to feel.

As the reported polls neared 80 percent, I accepted my fate and put my new power suit on. A few days prior, my big cousin, who is a fashion designer, picked out a nice pinstripe pantsuit and a bright orange blouse. Orange is the color that represents the sacral chakra. The center of one's creativity and synchronicity. Three years later, I'd use this chakra to redefine how I showed up in the world in a way that allowed me to be soft, strong, and vulnerable, free from armor. This loss would be the beginning of my ability to be in more control of who I was and how I gave myself to the world. Still in my twenties, when I ran for office, I had yet to discover and know how to use my voice. When it came to other people, I always followed their program, even when I knew it wasn't what I wanted to do. I watched my inner child take the beatings from the world, triggered by events that happened to me long ago, and I didn't step in and affirm that what those other people said about me was not important. Truthfully, I cared too much about what they thought and internalized it all. It created the perfect environment for the personal hell I was itching to get out of.

That night, I walked into my party smiling ear to ear. I did the thing I set out to do, and I was beyond proud of the work my team accomplished. I was relieved it was over. I couldn't be happier; I was the luckiest loser. As ABC 7 covered successful election results, an interview with my opponent flashed across the screen. She was in shock and had tears in her eyes. I smiled, looking at her, feeling confident that this was as it should be. That night, I laughed deep belly laughs with my best friends, celebrated with old lovers, and showered love and gratitude upon all those that held my hand along the way, guiding me to this moment. I left that night having no regrets.

My campaign stretched me in ways I never knew were possible. The time in which it happened, the eve of my thirtieth birthday, catapulted me into a new state of being, understanding, and existing. In this new life, I realized I had choices. I could make them based on a range of factors, but ultimately, I had to confirm what I decided honored me, protected me, and made me feel whole.

Despite my altruistic motives to serve my community, a conviction I have to this day, I ran because I wanted, needed, to be liked, to be loved, to be favorited. People that run for office have some codependent tendency that is a cry for help. For me, I had lived my life doing everything "perfect" so that I would always stay in the good graces of those who showered me with love and affection, those that I felt accepted me. And the premise of a campaign is to be favorited enough, get the votes, and win! I had to be likable, amendable to their wants and needs, and say all the right things. Thus, the unrelenting hunger fed off every knock on the door and every vote cast.

It became my driving force. Be dragged in the mud, keep going. Hear rumors about having your core team compromised, keep going. I couldn't rock the boat. I had to win, even if the foundation was faulty. So the moment mommy asked me that simple question, just two days before Election Day, I paused and assessed all that had transpired, all I had done, all I learned, and how it made me feel. Finally, an opportunity for the truth: I did not feel good. The drive exhausted me.

So, I was left with a choice: win at all costs, even at my expense, or choose myself and explore more of the life that was waiting for me. Mommy's gentle question was a word from God, tapping deep into the recesses of my being, flowing past the ego front I put up and got to the heart of the matter, my heart.

And I said no.

Not like this. Indeed, being liked and accepted is part of the human journey, and it comes at a cost, but this was a cost I was not willing to pay. And when this decision settled into my spirit, it signaled the Universe to meet my needs another way, a safer, more whole way, because this wasn't it. Knowing now what I didn't know then, this choice was rooted in being abundant, in knowing that saying no to this would be saying yes to more, to something else, to something more glorious, more divine. My yes would signal to Spirit that I was ready to cocreate something more marvelous than I had ever imagined, something that came with ease, made me feel good, and not empty and low in the process.

To be clear, I'm not saying being in office would be a bad experience for me in general. I am offering a revelation that the intention and foundation from which I pursue the things I want in the world informs how I experience it. I believed that running for office would guarantee my acceptance, and I'd be liked. These were my expectations, and I am confident I would have been miserably disappointed to find that the deep abyss of need was still there, hungrily waiting for me to consume anything and everything to satiate it unsuccessfully. Therefore, if I were to do it again, my only expectation would be to experience and be present and welcome whatever came my way.

It took me nearly three years to accept that I lost my election. Whenever I spoke about my experience, I always referenced the newfound awareness and learnings I earned, never able to utter that I lost. It was hard. It stunk of rejection and forced me to accept it as my reality.

I lost.

Not a bad loss, in fact, a most valiant loss. But a loss is a loss. I lost my election. I lost the version of me that believed I needed to seek outside myself for love and acceptance. I lost the conviction that acceptance and likability had to be painful, and if I compromised myself just enough, it would eventually pay off. I lost showing up as a people pleaser. I was once always willing to support and fix someone's problem in hopes that one day when I needed help, they would be there for me to count on.

By accepting this loss, I made space for gain. I gained the courage to speak up when reciprocity in relationships was nonexistent. I attuned my ear to listen and trust myself when I felt something. I could say "ouch" when it hurt, especially when it came from people I loved and cared for. I would proceed forward with a decision after checking in with myself. I gained a newfound appreciation for my ability to sustain myself and love myself deeply. This allows me to make space for others who genuinely loved me for me; whose love isn't conditional or requires me to acquiesce on something important to me. I gained confidence in my voice to speak up and refuse the abuse of others, regardless of whether it made them like me less or incited vexation. And most importantly, I know what love and acceptance feel like and confidently reject offerings that were the opposite.

My choice to say no and yes to more, albeit the unknown, was the most autonomous decision I've ever made. No longer intoxicated with the drive to be externally filled and validated, it was the first sober choice I made when I approached the crossroads my path led me to. *"Do you really want this?"* And with intentional communion with myself, I chose an abundant life.

SHARED WOMB, SHARED WOUNDS

My sister Jerrell taught me everything I know. I looked up to her. When I was a toddler and had to transition from baths to showers, she got in with me, so I felt less afraid. The powerful surge of water was no match for her presence. She soothed me. She taught me how to ride a bike and how to swim. When she was in middle school, a very gifted student, she came home and taught me all her lessons from the day. I'll never forget what a noun and a verb are. Her preparation and big sibling due diligence gave me the confidence to excel in Language Arts and beyond.

My sister is five years older than me. Mommy and my sister's father were divorced, we think, when I was born. On paper, most would say we were half-sisters because we had different fathers, but that all goes out the window when you've shared the same womb.

During our childhood, my sister took to the performing arts; she was a natural performer. When she gave an oratorical performance, there was never a dry eye. Her recitation of James Weldon Johnson's "The Creation" always earned a standing ovation. She added the appropriate inflection for the voice of God. You would have thought she stood with God as the Earth formed land and sea. As an eighth grader, she started a performing arts troupe, Young Talented Children (YTC), with students throughout the school. We traveled across the city to perform original productions from her very own imagination. My sister had adults that encouraged her creativity surrounding her. She made a B-Line to the performing arts program when she transitioned to high school. Every year we looked forward to seeing her on the stage, often starring as the lead. Her precocious pursuit of enrichment opportunities to fill her time and enhance her already gifted creative prowess rubbed off on me as I was her trusted sidekick.

My sister and I had the typical sibling relationship. Wherever she went, I had to go. We fought like a married couple when we weren't tied at the hip. As the big sister, she liked to punk me. I hated when mommy left the two of us alone at the house. Every time, without fail, my sister would have it out for me. For the longest, I wondered if I was guilty of something other than being a pesky, spoiled little sister. When I wasn't her sidekick, I doubled as my mommy's shadow, and I learned that this didn't always sit well with my sister.

Mommy and I had a unique, nearly inseparable bond. My sister and mommy didn't have what we shared. Mommy and I laughed, joked, and delighted in the same foods. During car rides, I sat up front with her, with my sister in the back. Even though Jerrell anticipated the arrival of her baby sister, the novelty had worn off as mommy and I spent more time together. My sister's misplaced frustration came out with her mean comments or her hits and punches to my body. Mommy saw it and would break up our bouts, if need be, but she largely stayed out of it. I was never quite sure why my sister held animosity toward me. Years into adulthood, my sister finally told me it was because mommy and I were so close, and she felt left out. Nevertheless, I didn't wait decades for her to stop; our physical feuds were going to end on my terms.

Our final duel was like the final fight scene between Deebo and Craig in the hood classic *Friday*. Deebo is the neighborhood bully. Whenever he came on the block, a menacingly eerie song accompanied his heavy steps. As Deebo roamed the streets, heading toward an unsuspecting target, his body hulked over his next victim, casting an intimidating shadow that dwarfed their entire body. Craig and his sidekick Smokey made wisecracks about Deebo but always cowered in Deebo's face. For so long, I envisioned laying my sister clean out, thinking about the right combination of moves powerful enough to put her in her place.

Then it finally happened.

It happened one afternoon when all three of us were home, mommy, Jerrell, and me. My sister pushed up on me one good time, and I must have taken a pill that turned me into the Hulk because I started swinging and wailing on her until she fell back on our second-hand Lay-Z-Boy recliner. My mommy heard the commotion and came to break it up. But once she saw the vigor behind my every blow, she waited a few seconds to let me savor my moment. Then she pulled me off my sister. I stood back and looked down at her. The smirk on my face said it all. "You got knocked the fuck out!" That was the last time my sister laid a hand on me.

Some mornings in our apartment on Green St. were peaceful. I don't remember those much. I just know that my sister made her way to high school, and I walked to the bus stop a few blocks away to go to Beasley, a prominent magnet public school. Then there were those chaotic mornings. Once my sister's progress reports revealed just how much progress, or lack thereof, she was making, mornings almost always featured a brawl between her and mommy. These mornings accentuated by screams and threats for my sister to get out of bed and get ready for school, to mommy physically dragging her from her bed toward the bathroom. Each tug at my sister poured an ounce of resentment into her heart. Each scream pushed my sister further and further out of the house until she was old enough to leave on her own.

My mommy was doing the thing she thought best. When she saw the path my sister was heading down, she saw herself: defiant, lacking zeal for life, and despondent. Mommy fought with her mama all throughout her life; they disagreed on everything from the high school mommy would attend to mommy's hairstyles and how to cover up her alopecia as a middle school kid. During those fretful mornings, with every tug, mommy frantically grabbed hold of the parts of her that my sister inherited. They were the parts that would result in years of mistakes and dead ends. Mommy hoped to scream away the whispers that planted seeds of confusion, disorganization, and rebellion. She thought if she applied enough force, the only tool she had, the only one she learned and experienced in her interactions with her mama, she could steer my sister toward a path brighter and easier than hers with fewer setbacks.

But it didn't work. My sister's estrangement morphed into a huge block between mommy and her, and her and me, and my sister and our home, limiting my memories with my sister during those times. Jerrell spent a lot of time away with her friends. My sister sought refuge at her best friend's home and stayed out late, despite knowing that a guaranteed fight would ensue upon her return. Things were different. We didn't hang out like we used to, but when I could tag along with her or hang with her friends, I relished those moments. Whenever my sister showed attention, I held on to it. When she graduated from high school and turned eighteen, she spent a semester away for college, came back to Chicago, but never returned to our home on Green St.

With my sister out of the house and my mommy's transitions between reality and her altered states, I doubled down on my independence and quieted any concerns or cries for help. Every morning I witnessed the showdown between my sister and mommy, I committed to never be a problem. I stayed out of the way. I took care of my schoolwork. I participated in extracurricular activities. I kept up with important deadlines. If I needed my mommy's signature or money, I'd let her know what it was for and how much. Those tumultuous mornings told me to keep my shit together and be perfect. I wanted none of the smoke festering under mommy's surface.

This resolve helped me control my relationship with mommy. As long as I was perfect, we would be good. I didn't want the disappointment, the fits or screams that came from a mistake, or simply dropping the ball for being a kid. While my physical survival needs were met, emotionally and mentally, I felt like I was on my own. Children growing up in the same home can respond to the same environment in different ways. My sister and I shared the same mom, and our fathers were equally estranged and consistently inconsistent. What I saw around me motivated me to double down on doing life another way. My sister and I responded differently to our wounds and environment, a varied combination of avoidance, silencing, and disassociation. She didn't have the luxury of having the same view that I had.

In the following years, I sensed my sister's distance even more and tried to find ways to stay around her. Lessons I learned growing up told me the best utility to people is being needed. So, if I saw a need my sister had, I would do what I could to fulfill her need. In doing so, I would be near her. She would see value in me. As my sister embarked on her independent journey, I was there to help her along the way. When she moved to a new apartment, I visited and noticed that she could use some help keeping the place tidy. Without asking, I'd volunteer to clean up her entire place for free while she was out, helping her stay organized. As she explored her artistry, she and her friends started a music group, and I tried to be present at every performance. I was the supportive little sister, always looking up to her.

All throughout my giving, I looked for signs that she liked me and saw value in our relationship. When she confided in me, I took this as a sign that what I was doing was working. So when she called me and told me she was expecting her first child, I knew I had to be there with her every step of the way. I was a junior in high school, and she told me she was about three months pregnant. She asked me to keep it between us, and I was so thrilled to be in on her secret. After all, we grew up in a conservative Black Christian family, so having children out of wedlock was not others looked down upon. My sister started avoiding the family, and when she did come around, she did silly things like holding up a magazine in front of her belly while sitting down. When my mom suspected something and asked me if I knew anything, I always denied it, never compromising my sister's confidence in me.

As the new baby grew in my sister's belly, so did the role I tried to fill in my sister's life. My opportunity to help lead the family in a new direction had come. I attended the city's best high school and would be the first in my family to attend college. My nephew would follow in my footsteps. I believed that because I had the capacity, I was responsible for training him the right way. After a challenging birth, he came to us on Saturday, July 7, 2007.

It felt good to be needed. As my sister's family grew, so did my support and love for them. With the arrival of my first niece, her second child, I solidified my role as super auntie. At the time, I was a third-grade math teacher, and I helped my nephew with his schoolwork, babysat, and took the kids on new adventures. In 2016, I won four tickets to the White

House Easter Egg Hunt, the final one of the Obama era. I was also halfway through my second master's degree at the University of Pennsylvania. I asked my sister if she and my nephew were interested in coming. Of course, they were. I bought his plane ticket and invited our little cousin who was his age. The four of us, clad in our Easter Sunday's best, headed to 1600 Pennsylvania Avenue. It was truly an experience. Because I had the privilege of seeing so much of the world, I wanted my sister's kids, my legacy, to have the same experiences. I wanted them to see that there was so much they could explore, and with the world's vibrant colors, they could paint their very own future, realizing their own reality on the blank canvas that life offered them.

As I poured from my cup, I never considered the precedent it set or that my well could run dry. I built my relationship with my sister based on the roles we assumed, the masks we wore, I the giver, and her the receiver. I saw myself the way my family saw me: young, decent career, expendable income, childless. I got caught up in the hype that having those things meant I didn't have need, or I wasn't as needy as my sister or anyone else who didn't have what I had. Most importantly, I believed I couldn't place the same expectations on my sister that she could have of me.

My sister wasn't the only person I stretched myself to convey utility. Over time, I realized as I ran from place to place, person to person to be needed, mistaking it for love and being valued, I exhausted myself. I saw that just as the shared wounds from our environment hurt my sister, it hurt me too and left me with a void I worked so hard to fill. Was I seeking to be mothered by the only other person who was a witness to what I experienced? Probably. She was an extension of my mommy, a more sober version I felt I could really speak to and who heard me. Nevertheless, the day came when I finally looked at myself in the mirror and saw the mask I donned for so long. It was almost unrecognizable from my skin, deeply embedded in the open wounds I worked so hard to fill with everything and everyone else.

I remember sitting on Dr. Ali's (my former therapist) couch one afternoon in December 2019.

"We only talk when I call her."

I wanted a real friendship with my sister. When we talked, we spent time catching up with one another, but I realized it was always me who dialed out, always me who came to visit her in the suburbs. I was furious when she showed up at family gatherings empty-handed, came late, left early or late, barely, if ever, lifting a finger to help clean up. Meanwhile, I assumed a *matriarch in training* role and helped coordinate family dinners, often spending more money than a family of one should contribute. I thought this was what I was supposed to do.

I didn't like the way this one-sided, nonreciprocal relationship made me feel, and things had to change. I knew I couldn't control how my sister behaved. I couldn't change how anyone else in the family enabled it as well. I could only change my response, and that meant stemming the flow from my cup.

Whenever my sister planned a family trip, I'd jump on and join them if I was available. In August 2020, things were reopening after the first wave of the COVID-19 pandemic, and we wanted to take advantage of affordable airfare. She set her eyes on Denver to celebrate her wedding anniversary and scout out the next location for her yoga hiking retreat. Denver was on my list, and I was eager to go. As we identified potential Airbnb's and crafted the itinerary, we discussed who should pay for what.

"So, if we get this Airbnb, how about you pay for 40 percent, and we'll pay 60 percent? We'll buy food for the house for breakfast, so it should net out. And as we looked at rental cars, it costs more for an extra row since you're another person, you should pay half of the rental car."

Forty percent? Half? It's just me.

When she said this, it took me aback. Here I am, one person, and you're asking me to pay way more than my fair share on the lodging and transportation when sharing with a family of five. I heard that voice yelp inside me, the one that realized we only talked when I called, the one that knew I couldn't expect my sister to show up for me the way I showed up for her. The one that knew I created this way of doing things.

"Okay."

I agreed to this arrangement, but something felt off. I had some extra money, so I knew I could afford it, but it still didn't sit well with me. I had a second thought about getting my own car and lodging, but I figured I was getting a deal by splitting costs with my sister. As our departure date neared, I asked my sorority sister, Ashley, to join me on the trip. She's an avid traveler, and I knew she could get up at a moment's notice.

I purchased my plane ticket and scheduled to get in that morning. I picked up the rental car and made the hour-long drive to our Airbnb. I'd have to come back that evening to pick up my sister and her family. Once I arrived, I settled into the house. I picked a room with a bathroom Ashley and I could share. Considering we were staying with a whole family and contributing a significant portion of the costs, I selected the room I wanted. I picked up the family that evening and made it back to the house. The next day, we planned to hike the Rockies. Ashley was getting in that morning, and we'd head there once she arrived.

The next morning, we cooked breakfast, and the kids got started with virtual learning. There was an odd energy in the air. My sister complained their bed was uncomfortable and made a snarky comment about me sleeping comfortably. I shrugged it off and got dressed. I rushed to the airport to pick up Ashley because we planned to leave for the mountains once we got back. But when I returned, we still weren't ready to leave. I'm not sure why it took so long, but we didn't leave for the Rockies for another three hours. I was furious and embarrassed because I had a guest. Considering it was early fall, we only had a few hours until dusk, and who wants to be in the mountains with mama and baby moose and bears at dusk?

While we waited, Ashley and I sat in the backyard and caught up. My sister came up to me and mentioned how this was actually a trip for her, and that they deserved to have the master bedroom. I told her I thought we should have that room because we're two women, and it didn't make sense to share a bathroom with her husband and her family. She didn't see it that way, and she pushed for me to switch bedrooms with her. I so desperately wanted to mention how I was unfairly paying more than I should for the trip, and I, too, deserved the nice bedroom, especially since they made a mess of the entire house and we'd barely been there for a day. But I couldn't. I didn't feel confident to say my truth. I didn't want to have a conflict. But here we were, having a conflict, and all I could do was simmer underneath my placid surface. I couldn't believe she asked me to pack up all my stuff and move into a bedroom where she had all her personal effects sprawled across the room.

Here I was, having made significant concessions by contributing to this trip, and the one luxury I do have, she's taking from me. I was furious but also very hurt. After everything I had done for her, my sister wanted any and everything I had to offer. She wanted more money from me than was equitable. She wanted a bed and an en suite bathroom, the one thing that made me comfortable when she and her family took over the entire house.

"I knew I should have gotten my own place."

Then she mocked me.

"Now, don't get so bent out of shape. It's not that serious. This trip is about us. It's my anniversary." It was always about her. She made her kids everyone's responsibility. She had kids, so people should do that, offer that, buy that.

But it was *that* serious. It was always about her. I should have seen this coming. As I stared at her, I finally saw the truth. I saw my sister would stop at no end to take from me what gave her comfort. And she knew I wouldn't protest it. Instead of fighting, I decided to flee. I packed my bags and set them at the door. When we returned from the Rockies, I decided instead of staying another night, I was going to leave. Fueled by anger and feeling abandoned, Ashley and I made reservations at a nearby hotel and booked another Airbnb for the remainder of our trip. We left that night while the house slept. I felt exhilarated. I didn't speak with my words, I spoke with my actions, and which was the best I could do at that time.

The next morning, the original plan was to go to the only Black-owned yoga studio in Denver for class. I saw my sister and instantly felt bad for what I had done. I did more than ruffle feathers. I broke the unwritten agreement that our respective roles dictated for our relationship. What did I do wrong? Stand up for myself and left. I stood up for myself with my feet. My bold action made a clear statement: I had nothing left to give.

It's been nearly two years since that day, and my sister and I have yet to have a candid conversation about what happened or the state of our relationship. My family has many unspoken rules. One of them is never to discuss the problems you have with other people. You just hold on to them for decades and flip out every time you're triggered.

After Denver, I spent months trying to sit down with her to explain my side. But eventually, I leaned into being misunderstood, letting time grow around that moment. I own my decision to leave because I made it clear I was no longer giving to her and demanded respect for who I was and my contributions to the family. I stopped giving so much. I took off the mask that had become like skin and tended to the wounds that made me believe I had no choice but to give until the love and acceptance came.

Instead of seeing my resources as easily expendable and a pawn to keep people around me, I saw them as valuable. They had to be earned by those I was in a relationship with, regardless of who they were to me. I had to honor that value by practicing discernment and knowing who I could expect from and those I couldn't. I couldn't make giving conditional either. If I gave to someone, it didn't give me the right to expect from them. That's what hurt me most with my sister. I figured after all I had done, she'd at the very least make a concession for me. But that wasn't what our roles dictated for us.

What I was left with was a sister who I deeply loved but couldn't get through to. I realized there was more to what went on that I will never see, a truth from her that she could never put into words. I also had to accept that she would have to be misunderstood.

Trauma bonds and the people we grew up to be in that environment nurtured our relationship. The trauma left deep wounds in each of us, and we took up specific roles to compensate for our lack. However, as I started to identify and address my own needs and not seek their fulfillment from others, I realized the old contract no longer fit who I was becoming. I was becoming someone who didn't identify with her troubled past and evolved into someone who could transcend and alchemize it. I became someone who knew that better was somewhere beyond taking the scraps that folks offered or begging them to show up in a way that made me feel good. I became someone who believed she wasn't missing out if I rejected a conditional relationship.

My sister and I are not where we used to be, and that's as it should be. We are evolving into the people we needed in our darkest moments. As we continue in our growth, I notice we are growing back together, but with stronger roots. These roots can sustain our respective needs, so we grow healthy branches that extend toward each other in love, ease, and grace. With these branches, we can willfully and gracefully embrace who we've become, the best whole and perfect versions of ourselves.

MAMA GOTTA HAVE A LIFE, TOO

> *There's only one thing harder than accepting this, and that is not accepting it.*
> —BYRON KATIE, LOVING WHAT IS: FOUR QUESTIONS THAT CAN CHANGE YOUR LIFE

"What would it mean for your mom to have her own experience?" The words struck me. Dr. Ali, my first therapist, posed the question to me. As we inched toward the end of my second session, she had heard enough to assess why I was there. Not just in her office, but why I was in this place in my life. It was January 2017, and something in me broke. For the life of me, I couldn't understand why all my relationships weren't working out the way I wanted them to. Did I set reasonable expectations for those close to me? Did I ask for too much? What were reasonable expectations, anyway? I knew I had good relationships with other people, but they were good on their terms. As long as I accommodated what they needed from me, we were all good. But when it came time to accommodate my needs, the good stopped flowing. I picked up this pattern early on, and I adapted. I learned to quiet the parts that wanted and needed more. Until I realized after all I had done, I was empty, unsatisfied, and didn't have anything to show for all my giving. Not from the folks I needed to show me the most love.

"She won't survive without me."

I was sure that if I didn't step in to help slay my mommy's dragons and even use my own sword at times, she'd be toast. That was my truth, and I couldn't chance it. I loved my mommy too much to have her out here like that. As my mommy altered her state, our mother-daughter relationship became codependent, and she reached to me to care for her in ways she could not do for herself. Her alterations numbed her from this reality as she coped through life's bouts of challenges and setbacks. I believed if I was capable, no matter the expense, I would do it for her, supporting her emotionally and materially. My assumed role was to help my mommy survive.

My mommy was born on Chicago's west side to Stanley and Lorriane Hale. She was the middle child, the first and only baby girl. She had a beautiful, freckled face and petite frame. A dazzling smile and a cackle that could locate her in a crowded stadium. Through hard work, discipline, and commitment, my Granna purchased their very first home, moved her family out of the projects, and relocated to Chicago's South Side. Her husband, my mommy's dad and my grandfather was city employee, working at the Chicago Transit Authority and the Chicago Police Department. He made good money, but Granna rarely saw any of it. Between cleaning *White folks' homes* and working at the Chicago Housing Authority, she saved enough money for a down payment. Grandpa Stanley, a man I've never met but have heard many stories about, was an avid gambler. He'd spend his check at the track and compromised his family's needs. Those impacts reverberated into the core of his children. His choices kept him from his family. They never knew what he really thought of them, whether he really loved them. At his funeral, my mommy was surprised to learn all her daddy talked about with his work friends was his baby girl, Ronda. She learned of his love for her posthumously.

Much of my mommy's story is tucked deep within her heart. I know early on, she set about the world not feeling confident to speak up for her needs, let alone understand that she had them and that they could be met. Since her adolescent years, she battled with mild alopecia. Her condition wasn't properly cared for. Confusion, fears, and tears about losing her hair were silenced and covered with a wig. There was no conversation, no explanation for why, no affirmation that she was still beautiful, and that her freckles made her shine. Tormented by classmates, she carried the burden of social exclusion like an albatross. Mommy looked to her mama for validation, security, softness even, just to know that it was okay for her to feel. Yet, each time she hoped for it, it never came. Her wants, wishes, and desires eclipsed by the "mother knows best" iron fist my Granna wielded. My mommy retreated and buried the need for attention deep inside. Altering her state numbed her and made her forget her woes, at least for a while.

Mommy's resolve was a volley of resentment and rebellion, mixed with attempts to seek her mama's approval and extend herself when asked or expected. This addictive cycle of maternal castigation and approval seeking became the blueprint of mother-daughter relationships in our family. Daughters would diligently seek softness and nurturing from their mothers, hoping to be enough, offer enough, silence enough, serve enough, placate enough. But it would never be *enough* to get what they really wanted and needed. At some point, every daughter realizes the cycle for what it is and that what they really want won't come. With no end in sight, the daughter must decide to continue, hoping they will one day be enough, or accept what is and seek validation on their own terms. At the other end of the pendulum, daughters who lived *their* mother's living years unsuccessfully seeking the warmness of their mother, made their love and acceptance conditional to their daughters when they became mothers.

Mommy's quest for her mama's approval and acceptance came with a set of sobering consequences. Seeking Granna's approval meant adopting a prescribed image she wanted mommy to portray. It meant mommy's life choices were dictated by Granna's desires for her life, not what mommy wanted. Consequently, mommy didn't develop the confidence to trust herself when she made a choice, especially if it wasn't what her mama wanted. Because she lacked this confidence, she didn't make the most responsible choices. As it would follow, mommy's silenced needy voice grew in size, and it would be her legacy who would have to answer the call.

Cars and transportation play a huge role in my family. Having reliable transportation is a necessity, especially when field travel is a work requirement. For much of my childhood, my mommy experienced difficulties maintaining reliable transportation. Consequently, for her to have a car, it had to be put in someone's name without existing infractions. My young perceptive eyes saw mommy's need and wanted to help. I assumed that risk as a child who couldn't drive. I knew it was something my mommy needed, especially to get around to provide for our family.

I remember a time when I was about twelve years old, and our car was in one of Chicago's western suburbs impounds. Because the car was in my name, I had to be there to retrieve it. My uncle dropped mommy and me off at the tow lot, and I had to sign for the car and pay to get it back. I stepped up to the window and inquired about our car. The man looked at me, and I felt sadness and pity in his gaze. He told me the cost of releasing our car. Mommy handed me cash, and I counted it out, and we were a few dollars short. He took what I offered and gave me the keys and pointed me in the direction of the car. I walked away from the window toward my mommy and handed her the keys. We didn't talk about it. We never talked about anything we should discuss.

It was in this instance that I knew something wasn't right. I didn't know what to do. I didn't know what options I had other than to oblige to what my mommy needed. My intuition bubbled up inside of me, but I quieted these concerns and stayed at my mommy's side. Despite what I thought, it was clear my mommy needed saving. And if I was capable, I was going to do what needed to be done. Besides, doing what she needed me to do guaranteed that I would get the love and support of my mommy, and she would be here to provide it for me. However, as the years rolled by and parking tickets arrived with my name on them, it was something I could no longer ignore. And though my mommy had her challenges, they wouldn't be solved at my expense. I wasn't sure what her other options were, but I could no longer be one. So finally, with all my might and courage, I railed against this one-sided agreement and got the cars out of my name. Eventually mommy figured out alternative solutions to her dilemma.

"What would it mean for your mother to have her experience?"

"I did something really bad. And I don't know what to do."

I had just arrived home for my Thanksgiving break during my sophomore year of college. Not too long ago, my Granna gifted me her old 1997 red Pontiac Grand AM. Granna was a successful Mary Kay Senior Sales Director and earned the Grand AM when she became a director. She wanted me to have a car as I was in college, but she wanted to make sure I put it in my name even though the car was still under her insurance policy. Although the car was mine, I didn't take it to school with me. Mommy needed a car. After completing my midterms, I was happy to be home to celebrate my favorite family holiday.

My mommy was curled into a ball on the edge of the couch in our family room.

"I was driving, listening to music, and got distracted. I ran through a stop sign and hit a car."

For most people, while this is an inconvenience, calling the police, filing a report, and making an insurance claim is the solution to this problem. But because mommy didn't have her license, she fled the scene. When she got home, she realized the front license plate was missing. She knew it would come back to her. Fresh off the Megabus, I jumped into crisis resolution mode, thinking of scenarios to get us out of this jam. I don't know who offered the suggestion, but it made sense I would take the fall for it since I could legally drive. If my mommy confessed, she would certainly head to jail, and that wasn't something we could afford.

The next day we went to the police station near the crash. The woman who was hit made a police report, and the officers drew a sketch of the driver from what she could remember. The sketch had an afro. I had locs at the time. I saw the image and seethed inside. I couldn't believe I was doing this. The officer asked me why I fled the scene. I told her I was nervous and didn't want to get in trouble. The truth was I was still on campus in Ann Arbor, Michigan, packing to come home for the holiday. The officer filed the appropriate report and attributed me as the perpetrator. They scheduled a court date during my Christmas break.

Next up was to tell my grandparents. Mommy had already shared the news with them. My Granna was surprised at what I did.

"Baby, you know we have car insurance, right? It's okay if you get into an accident. That's what it's for."

I hung my head in shame, knowing damn well I'd never do what my mommy did.

"I know. I was just nervous. It won't happen again."

I returned home for Christmas break and attended traffic court a month later. Neither my mommy nor I knew what the charges were, but they were pretty bad, which could have resulted in jail time and a big fine. Luckily, my court-appointed attorney was a Michigan graduate, and when it came time for my case, she made a motion, the judge agreed, and it was over.

"Go Blue!" she said. We parted ways.

Even though it was over, the brevity of the infraction hung over my head like a pregnant storm cloud. It's the only infraction I have on my record. When I ran for office, I wondered if it would come up and if my opponents would use it to discredit me. I was on pins and needles, waiting for that cloud to burst. By the grace of God, it never did. By now, enough time has passed for it to clear from my record, but it's something I think about every now and again, the depths I was willing to go to save my mommy and how far she'd let me. The decisions I made as a child, I had no business doing so. I was supposed to be under the care and supervision of an adult, my mommy. I should have been under her protection. Instead, I experienced a glimpse of the world that alters life trajectories, ruins futures, that maims and scars. My mommy's shortcomings forced me to be the adult.

That Grand AM never got back on its feet after that hit and run. A few months later, it was parked in a precarious place, and someone hit it, and the driver ran. Go figure. It was deemed totaled and inoperable. Although it was my first car, I never got the full privilege of having it to myself.

I can't recall what mommy did after that, but it would be a few years until I had another set of wheels, ones that I paid for myself.

As a recent college graduate, I enrolled in a teacher training graduate program. Throughout the week, I had to go to the west side to teach, Monday through Thursday, then go to class downtown on Fridays. At the time, my best friend Brianna was preparing for a graduate program abroad in Austria. She had a car passed down from her eldest sister to get around. As she prepared to leave, I asked her parents if I could buy it from them. They agreed and even accepted my term of installment payments. The day arrived for my best friend's departure, and I could set sail on my own new adventure. Every day I drove to the west side, blasting my favorite tunes down the expressway. But this newfound excitement and freedom had its limits because mommy didn't have her own car.

What was mine was ours. She asked me to borrow my car when I most likely needed it. I said I didn't mind because I was used to taking public transit. Weekends were tough because when I wanted to hang out with friends, even though I had a car, I had to ask mommy to drop me off so she could do what she needed to do, or worse, ask a friend to drop me off. The voice I once silenced, now a muffled grunt, and it asked me to turn inward. How did this make me feel? It pointed out the deep resentment I harbored toward my mommy. I never liked these setups. I hated that my mom put me in the position and asked anyway. It was hard to say no to her. I never felt like I had a choice.

This voice pointed to the immense resentment I harbored toward mommy. It left me wondering whether I'd do something about it. Every time I got in my car, I was furious. There was always something of hers I needed to clean up, reminders of her taking advantage of me and taking what she needed from me, disregarding what would be kind and considerate to me. I had no boundaries, and she knew that. Despite all this, I kicked off the pattern of worrying too much about mommy's ability to get by. I didn't trust that what I felt was enough to stand on its own and make it all stop. I had too much fear of losing my mommy's love. This rodeo went on for some time until God said it was enough.

It was Easter Sunday, 2013, and we returned from dinner at my Granna's house. Whenever my mom used my car, it would, without a doubt, be a mess. On top of that, you'd see more of her things in there than mine. She had completely taken over, and I felt so stuck and hurt. So in my passive-aggressive way, cleaning the car and removing her stuff was my protest against our existing arrangement. On this particular day, I felt compelled to take nearly everything out of the car; most of our personal effects, except my favorite CDs. After I tidied up the car and brought everything into the house, I prepared for the workweek. My mom grabbed the keys to run a quick errand. The car didn't have a remote control, so you had to use the key to lock the doors. In her hasty return, she left the key in the driver's side door and ran inside. Not long after, she looked for the key to run back to the car. She instantly realized her mistake, stepped outside, and I heard a loud shriek.

"Lotus! The car is gone. Call the police." I ran downstairs, and she wasn't lying. The car was, in fact, gone. She admitted leaving the keys in the car.

"That was all we had," she lamented, tears streaming from her eyes.

I was in shock and disbelief but didn't emote much. I called the police and made a report. Going into instant crisis resolution mode, I asked my coworker to pick me up at the train station. The next few weeks were agonizing being back on public transit. The police found my car down the street, and it was involved in a hit and run. After clearing that with the insurance company, I received my insurance claim to get a new car. Mommy offered me three thousand dollars towards a new car. After that experience, things shifted significantly. My mommy respected that this car was mine. And though I let her drive it when she needed to, it wasn't as if it had been before. I wish I could say I had enough, but I didn't. It wouldn't be another four years until I reached the boiling point, and the voice inside, no longer a muffle, but a roaring wrecking ball, put the abuse to a halt.

"What does it mean for your mother to have her experience?"

This question forced me to wrestle with the truth. The truth was I spent so much of my life, at no fault of my own or anyone else's, living for my mommy rather than myself. Honestly, living for everyone else but me. I didn't make decisions that were better for me, and my inaction enabled mommy to manipulate and take advantage of me. The adult I needed all those years had to show up; the adult I wished expressed how dumb it would be for me to confess to a crime I didn't do; the adult I wished had asked mommy to find another way to get to and from work; the adult that asked me to ask myself if I was really okay with what was happening and encourage me to make a choice that was fair to me. I acknowledged the harm of my inaction and extended myself much-deserved grace. The parent within me was awakening, and her primary objective was to take care of Lotus.

When I finally said no and chose for myself, I didn't know what the future held for mommy or me. But I knew it had to be better than my existing reality. In my reparenting and healing journey, I had to reorient myself in my body, trust what I felt was true, and dig deep on courage to manifest it in the world around me. This is an ongoing process. One that constantly stretches me and commands me to recommit time after time. In this process, I revisit past traumas I endured and give light to them. Putting them on paper has been therapeutic beyond belief. Through my writing, I witness my past and affirmed the version of me who survived, and accepted that what happened was my truth, instead of avoiding it.

It is also true that, though my mommy was on the other side of those traumas, she was doing her best to survive. She had her own traumas to bear, and she needed someone else, me, to help carry her burdens. She, too, had a life to live and needed to get by the best she could. She, too, was seeking the very thing we all need to get by in this world: love and acceptance.

Allowing my mommy to have her own experience meant I couldn't worry about what that experience would include. I cannot bear the brunt of responsibility or manipulate the outcome by overextending myself. It also meant choosing myself was worth more than what would be withheld from me. The love I hoped to receive was only conditional. I wanted a love that accepted me in my full expression.

As I have allowed my mommy to have her own experience, she has come alive. Just the other day, I told her how proud I was of her and that she was indeed growing up. As I decided to no longer be responsible for her, she is now in a position to care for herself, make mistakes, and rebound from them. We all need our own experiences to learn from them and grow in confidence. So that one day, we can use our voice to say yes, no, or not right now. This confidence allows us to safely have our own lived experiences and live a life we're proud of.

GOD IS LOVE IS LOVE

"I think I like a girl."

I finally said it. I said what I had been obsessing about over the last few weeks.

I shared this with my sister, the first person I ever told. It was May 2020, and little signs of life were popping up after an abrupt global shutdown. I was able to get some miles in the new car I leased in March, a week before the shutdown, and I was itching to see people and do anything. My sister and I made plans to go grab an ice cream and catch up.

"Ohhh, this is exciting!" my sister exclaimed. After birthing her third child, a COVID-19 era baby at that, any news that didn't have to deal with school closures or rising COVID-19 cases was juicy and exciting.

I realized I did, in fact, like a girl. *Do I like her? Why can't I keep her off my mind?* I often pondered. I then realized that given my experience in dating men, had she been a man, I would have no doubt that I liked her. Just acknowledging the reality of my truth felt pretty natural and normal. And finally, I no longer felt compelled to hide it from myself at this point in my life. Yet, what gave me pause was the implications of this affirmation. Could I actually date women? Indeed, this was a presumptuous thought. However, it was a reality I had to entertain, if only in my mind.

Sure, I've had *girl crushes* before; having a strong affinity toward attractive Black women because, not only was I an attractive woman, but the way we showed up in our skin appealed to me. But beyond our aesthetics, it was the influence we had on those near and far in our orbit, our vivacious laughter and magnetic personality, and how we poured into our gifts and talents that dazzled the world and left it better than we found it. When I met women like this, they were versions I hoped I could evolve into. I'd wonder and claim these women as someone I'd look up to and become close friends with, admire them and seek mentorship. This is why several of my close friends and confidants are at least fifteen years my senior. All things considered, I've never actually thought about dating them.

Notwithstanding, there have undoubtedly been many times when I was sexually attracted to women. Years before my declaration, my best friend Brianna, who remembered her truth a few years prior, asked me if I would date women, and I said that I wouldn't but could certainly see myself sleeping with them. She snickered and said, "I can see that." But she knew long before I wanted to admit it to myself. She just tested the waters. In that vein, I have always marveled at how beautiful the female body was. From voluptuous and curvy to slim thick physiques, God was intentional when He designed our bodies.

I like to say that my sexual evolution and how I came to date women is a process of remembering, as opposed to "coming out." As I am now engaged to a woman, memories of childhood interactions and attractions surface in the front of my mind. Remembering that I love women is like securing the cheat code that unlocked some underground lair of my identity, giving me the confidence I didn't know I was missing. These memories that pop up remind me of instances as a child when I knew I liked girls.

In second grade, my classmate Michelle was what most referred to as a tomboy. At the time, Usher just released his iconic song and video "My Way." Michelle had taken to the song and learned Usher's choreography, and she poured her whole seven-year-old soul into every move. I enjoyed watching her dance and sing the song, and I felt like she was talking to me. As I looked on as she performed, something in me felt good and satisfying. But then, there was something that would come later on to discourage me from this attraction. The thoughts said this was a forbidden feeling. In another instance, there was once a girl who I would kiss every so often. But as we got older, she told me this wasn't something we should be doing. As I matured, I continued to hide this part of me and ignore it when affection or attraction would arise.

As the years rolled by, I'd meet women whose pull of attraction was undoubtedly present and fiercely uncontrollable, but my automatic response was to ward it off like a virus, to shut down and avoid it at all costs. Even when I first publicly dated women, I had to remind myself that it was okay. From the childhood discouragement to my indoctrination of the conservative Christian values, I had mounted a hefty opposition to any idea related to same gender love. I remember hearing stories of a few choir directors at my childhood church that were asked to leave or step down from their position because they identified as LGBTQ. This reminded me that anything that wasn't by the book, the Bible that is, was shunned and forbidden. However, the moment I laid eyes on the first woman I dated, all the antagonizing and implicit self-deprecation fell away, and I could pursue the love that God had waiting for me the entire time.

I met a woman—I'll call her Sabrina—doing one of the things I'm most passionate about, leading a community and rising in a time of crisis. We connected on our shared interest to develop a mutual aid support network during the dark unknown days of the pandemic and subsequent shutdown. What started as a purely professional and friendly relationship catalyzed a self-evolution that would turn my entire world right side up.

What I enjoyed most about my relationship with Sabrina was that it was like nothing I had ever experienced, and therefore, I could show up in a new way. I have always been someone that has gone after what I wanted, and as Beyoncé pointedly proclaims in "Formation," when I see something, I want it. This drive I had would leave the men I dated intimidated, and any type of push deemed aggressive and not in the sexy *let me get on top* kind of way. But in my relationship with

Sabrina, and generally, in some same gender female relationships, the heteronormative rules were out the window. There was no *man* or *woman*. In fact, though I present as a very feminine woman, a girly girl, if you will, I have big *top* energy in my female relationships. When I share this with those close to me, they stop and wonder as I just bulldozed through what they thought was feminine and masculine. Whenever my mom asks who the man is, I always joke and say it's me. Straights are easy to get to. In many of my relationships with men, I've pursued them to keep things going or had to quiet a part of me that made them feel uneasy. But with women, my pursuit was out of pure adoration. The women accepted and encouraged it.

My relationships with women have been a place of nurturing and wisdom exchange. It offers the sage advice and sisterhood you find with your girlfriend and mentors, with a spice of romantic love and great sex. My relationships with women are a soft place to land. My decision to honor my truth has shifted many things I thought weren't possible in my life. It has allowed me to truly dream big and think expansively about the world I live in and how to make it mine. My choice to love who I love ushered me into deeper intimacy with myself: to speak up for the little girl inside, the little girl who shape-shifted for love, acceptance, and consideration. The love I got was conditional and based on what I could offer or accommodate. Me, as myself, wasn't enough.

Since I have taken steps to accept myself as I am, it has allowed me to take better care of myself and command the utmost respect. It allowed me to tap into the intuitive nature every human is blessed with and use that as my compass to guide me through life's challenges. Choosing this love reminds me to live in the duality of life, for when shit gets bad, life's love nectar is always sweet to the taste. To seek my own approval and not rely on that of others. My choice to love who I want to love compels me to seek the truth in every moment. It is grounding. It keeps me sane. And it reminds me that all is well. Love is abundant. And God has blessed us all with the capacity to give and receive. In this new state of being, I thank my ancestors for living their lives, docile and quietly, and those who lived loudly and unabashedly. I stand on their shoulders to be proud. I am eternally grateful to be a chalice to receive love from all types of sources and people.

We just finished one of those "massage me after a tough workout" sessions. It was a beautiful late Sunday summer morning in July. My former lover and I had just completed a dynamic HIIT (high-intensity internal training) workout at the park, and we came home to shower, share a meal, and chill. Although it was during the pandemic, the summer of 2020, I still maintained a disciplined workout regimen. And at the time, I was dating this woman who ate chickpeas and air, as I joked, so it wasn't hard to maintain a healthy lifestyle when we were together. I asked for a classic rub down, after which we ended up wrapped in each other's arms on my living room hardwood floor.

"There's no way this could be bad. How could God not bless this?"

I said, with tears streaming down my eyes. She wiped a new tear as the words fell from my lips. She wasn't new to the whirlwind of emotions, and subsequent reactions from family, that came once remembering who you were born to be and meant to love.

According to what the good Christians said, I was sure to burn in hell, but here I was lying with a beautiful woman and enjoying one of the best blessings and pleasures God gave us. I once kicked it with this guy whose "mood" playlist was "God is Good." I, at the time, was a judgey type Christian, thought it was blasphemous, but now after experiencing the beautiful pleasure of sex, I understood.

This love I've found, surely of God, is revolutionary. It nurtures the courage to tear down walls I've built to protect me, walls that society put around to control me. There's nothing like the power of love, and because it originates from God, the Supreme Being, and the source of all there is, it's perfect. Experiencing this love from God is different from the love the church preached and sang about.

My chase for God started early in my life. I went by the Good Book and feared perpetual doom if I stepped outside of what the Book told me to do. I judged myself and those around me and hid my deepest truth from myself because everything around me said it was taboo and not of God. I wrestled with my understanding of who God was and questioned God fiercely, and, at some point along the way, turned away from God. The Bible, in great detail, tortured, maimed, and ostracized women. This strict life did not accommodate for error. For years, I took this prescription. The side effects were my value, worth, and identity sewn into something I could not live up to. I remember the first time I had sex, something God created us to do. I was devastated.

I wondered, "What more could I offer a man now that I was no longer a virgin?" Surely believing I had fallen from God's grace.

Once I exhausted the fight to be something, someone that wasn't me, I fiercely questioned God. I took the space to learn more about how others lived their Christian faith. For them, it was freeing; it was grace in motion, their faith accommodated sex. My quest for the God I'd come to know and love made space for me to meet God in my Tarot Cards, in meditation and on my yoga mat, and in the ancient teachings of Buddhism, Hinduism, and Yoruba. I understood God existed in all these practices, and culture and geography gave God new names and origins. The truths I learned that existed in Christianity were present in all those other faiths. I marveled at how expansive God was so that all people, regardless of gender, where they called home, and the language they spoke, could embrace God and God's teachings. I knew that God could still meet me regardless of who I loved, the body parts they grew, and how they identified.

Society says healthy, bountiful relationships can only exist between a man and a woman. God did not bless anything else. But as I laid in this woman's arms, I wondered how God couldn't bless this. How could God create something so wonderful that happened naturally? Something so beautiful that it brought tears to my eyes, but it was not blessed. The natural feeling made sense to my body. Before I started having sex, I listened to many sex tales from women of all ages. Billions of dollars powered the music and porn industry about sex between men and women. This was ideal love and the only option. But when my turn to be with a man finally arrived, I felt like someone blew out my birthday candle and ran off with my cake.

"That's it?"

First, I wondered if it was me. Maybe I needed more experience for it to feel good. Maybe I should watch more porn so I'd know what I was doing and explore more of what could please me. I'm a doer, so I wanted to be in control of my pleasure so my partner would know what I needed. Yet and still, I noticed a trend after each new male partner. Most of my dating years consisted of me falling in love with a man and trying to do everything I could to earn requited love. Despite what I gave, the relationships always failed. They started off with love bombs and ended in the loss of erections.

I don't want to present as if same gender female relationships don't have issues because, regardless of gender, whenever you put two humans together, there will be conflict. But I didn't always think that. The connection between two women is so ethereal it made me think there was more intimacy, more depth than what was established. I assumed because my partner was a girl like me, she wouldn't dare hurt or manipulate me the way a man would. Maury said that was a lie. And I have the healed wounds to prove it. I had to develop boundaries to give me guardrails.

I had to understand this so my relationships could thrive. It's what I took into my current relationship, and it's these hard-learned lessons and appropriate timing that got me the ring resting on my finger. As I made my way through my remembering, I can say that I have experienced the love that God has for me through my beloved. What I've found is that the love I truly wanted, needed, was waiting for me in the arms of a woman with my name on it.

TRIBE

Be around the light bringers, the magic makers, the world shifters, the game shakers. They challenge you, break you open, uplift and expand you. They don't let you play small with your life. These heartbeats are your people. These people are your tribe.
—(DOBY 2018)

"I can't spend the summer here."

I pulled up to my house and turned off the engine. I sat with one leg outside the car and paused, finally, slowing down to think. Now four months into the pandemic, I was thankful we made it to the summer and had more facetime with the sun. I so needed it. But I knew the dreadful Chicago winter would soon return, and so would the ice-cold isolation we collectively weathered over the last few months.

I, like a lot of people across the globe, had the fortune of working remotely and could take my work anywhere. If I were going to do something different, now would be the time. But, if I'm honest, it wasn't just the pandemic that spurred my decision. I was going through my own transition, and an escape felt like the best option for me. As I sat with one foot in the car and one foot on the ground in front of my childhood home, I felt this overwhelming sense that I had to move. I had one foot timidly in my new life and one foot planted in my old life.

My idea of self, love, relationships, sexuality, and family were all evolving. I spent the last few years *doing the work*. I went to therapy, built new relationships and reprioritized existing ones, and accepted what is both good and bad. A total demolishment of who I once was. In partnership with my therapist, I developed coping strategies and set boundaries to reclaim myself, the parts that I gave so willingly to everyone and everything else. The difficult yet critical decision to choose myself time and time again signaled the universe to set a new pattern in my life, highlighted by new life chances and adventures. Shining with the novelty of a new life, I was still one foot in and one foot out.

The first person I told I would spend the winter abroad was my big sister Ebony. Ebony is about fifteen years older than me, and we met a few years ago when she ran for office. I heard she was a Michigan Wolverine, my alma mater, and a member of my sorority, so I had to meet her. We hit it off well and continued to nurture a friendship. Ebony lived a large and in charge dream big kind of life. She was a working mom and wife and still had the capacity to not only imagine her dreams coming true but to execute a plan and follow through. She offered me sound advice, wisdom, and the listening ear I needed at so many points.

Ebony is also one of those people that you have to watch what you say because she will hold you to it.

"So, are you still going on your trip? Have you made any plans?"

If anyone is going to hold me to my plans, it will be her. Though her question was pure, it felt like an indictment because I pretty much dropped the idea altogether. It was mid-October, and I hadn't even located my passport. Plus, I had no idea where I was going to go. It would be my first time going out of the country alone, and I didn't know anyone else who had done something like this. On top of all that, I felt pushed away from my home. Not by any person, but between the threat of violence, and the new person I was becoming, my old place was no longer a safe place to grow.

A few weeks later, Ebony and I celebrated my thirty-first birthday over dinner. With each passing day, I felt the ground beneath me become more precarious as I proceeded into this new life of unknown territory. In this new life, I spoke up for myself, I loved who I wanted to love, and I stopped doing the things that hurt me or allowed other people to hurt or disrespect me. It was heartbreaking because my family who knew me, my mommy, my sister, weren't coming along for my new journey. They were whose approval I sought and relished in. They were always rooting for me. But this new life, this new Lotus I was evolving into, they barely acknowledged that she, I, existed.

This new life I was walking into had dreams of a better, fuller life that satisfied me. She dared to have her cake and eat it too. But there's nothing worse than having all your dreams right before you, but you're too afraid of taking the leap toward them. At the time, I didn't know it, but I was getting closer to becoming a homeowner, but my limited belief in the impossible happening paralyzed me with fear. That evening at dinner, I cried in Ebony's arms because I desperately wanted more out of life. I felt the rub to vacate the old, but I lacked the faith.

"How can I do both?" I questioned. My confidence and faith were at an all-time low.

"It can happen." Ebony replied. Then she offered me the sign that I could physically hold on to. As I prayed to God to show his hand, it came in an envelope she handed to me: a fifty-dollar Airbnb gift certificate.

"I guess I'm going somewhere."

"Lotus!"

As I exited the Aruba International Airport, I heard a voice bellow my name. I was almost at a loss for words. Here I was, taking my first step into a new country, new continent, and someone knew my name. Though I'm pretty popular back home in Chicago and can almost always count on knowing someone else in any room, I didn't expect this.

"Lotus!"

I heard it again. I searched through the crowd of travelers pouring out of the airport, crossing the street in between cars, hugging loved ones, and heading to their rental cars. Then I landed on a bright, familiar face. It belonged to my Auntie Pat.

"You're not alone." I heard God whisper.

My Auntie Pat had been living in Aruba for a little over two years as a librarian at one of the local medical schools. She wasn't my blood relative. In fact, she was my sister's dad's older sister. Despite genetics, I grew up as a rightful member of the Hale Hill family. Blood doesn't always determine family. My tribe was a testament to that. I smiled and remembered my aunt did live here. And though I told her when I'd arrive, I didn't expect her to show up and greet me at the airport. It was the perfect affirmation that I made a good choice. During the plane ride, I had second thoughts and wondered if escaping was the right choice. I was in another country amid the only global pandemic anyone alive had ever experienced. I decided to escape because despite having my family come together to wish me a bon voyage, I felt very much alone in the world.

Before I heard Auntie Pat, my first greeter was the sun. Then I remembered the subzero temperatures in Chicago. With three months' worth of luggage, totaling nearly two hundred pounds, I galloped across the street and embraced my aunt. I was here. My Auntie Pat asked me if I needed help getting to my Airbnb. My "I can care for myself" reflex activated instantly. Old habits die hard. Based on my Airbnb host's advice, I had already downloaded the app to access a GPS map without internet access. I wasn't paying for an international plan for my three-month stay, so I had to be savvy.

Auntie Pat didn't insist and told me she'd meet with me that evening for a meal.

With my luggage in tow, I entered the car rental facility, waited for my car, loaded my cargo, and headed out of the parking lot. As I neared a very busy round-about, a traffic experience I had never had in the United States, I briefly doubted my decision to decline my aunt's help. Then I remembered that I'm from Chicago. So I tenaciously hopped right into oncoming traffic and made my way out of it. "I can do this!" I affirmed.

I made it to my Airbnb but noticed none of the homes had numbers on them. Open to exploration, I got out of my car and stood at the gate the GPS brought me to. I rang the doorbell, and a concrete sliding gate began to move. A lovely sun-kissed face greeted me, Naomi, the wife of my host family. I pulled into the carport area and jumped out of the car. Though COVID-19 was everywhere, I followed my urge to embrace her. She was so kind. She showed me to my studio, my home for this season. It was just as the pictures revealed. This warm welcome and beautiful home further confirmed my choice. I told her my aunt lived here and we'd be heading to dinner soon.

She exclaimed, "Oh, that's wonderful! I thought three months alone would be a lot for you. I'm glad you have someone here."

Was I the only one who didn't think what I was doing was abnormal? To be fair, I tend to do a lot of things most people won't ever do. People admired and encouraged me and called me courageous for taking risks and doing the hard things. Call it foolhardy, but I will jump right in, not always knowing the general rules. "Yeah, I'm glad she's here, too," I responded.

The following morning, I met my aunt for breakfast. Once we sat at our table, I spotted a young woman I met during my layover in Miami. This woman stood out to me because, like me, she was a young Black woman traveling alone. I eagerly introduced myself, and we exchanged information. She'd be here for a week and marveled at the idea of staying for as long as I planned to. When I saw her across the concourse, I was excited to have a friend, even for a short time. We made plans to meet at the world-famous Eagle Beach later that afternoon. Whenever I have peculiar occurrences or experiences I least expect, I always look to God and become curious about the purpose behind it. "You're not alone." I walked more confidently in my decision.

Years ago, I trained myself to "look for God in everything." When life shifted without explanation, I wondered how God was using the experience or circumstance to speak to or through me, transform me, or direct me. Seeing God in the world around me was a consistent prayer to see God's hand and cut away the fray, confusion, and ambiguity. And in moments like these, it reminded me I was not alone. God would show up through the people that came across my path. It emboldened my steps and comforted me.

Although I was having a completely new experience, I couldn't shake what wasn't there. Thoughts of who wasn't riding with me consumed me, and I hated it. At the time, I didn't understand the maxim that everyone can't go where you're going, even if they were family or your first friend. Prayerfully, I didn't have any expectations for my solo experience, so my time in Aruba revealed to me who my people were.

My tribe.

As I evolved into the new life destined for me, I needed my cloud of witnesses to surround and encourage me along the journey. These people would be my light-bearers who showed me their heart, illuminated the path ahead, and reminded me that I didn't have to be or do anything other than how I showed up. I didn't have to deny any part of me to be accepted and receive love or make them feel comfortable.

God was intentional about this process and my acceptance of what is. I didn't talk much with my family throughout my stay, particularly my mommy. Ordinarily, we spoke every day, but in this new season, we spoke about once a week, which isn't good or bad, just different, and that was the order of this new life, different. Being in a place with a change of pace allowed me to accept things as they came instead of trying to force them. I respected this break from my mommy as the distance and silence allowed me to put periods where I secretly hoped there would be a comma or ellipses, at the least. I hoped that my mommy would eventually come around to understanding and celebrating my newfound confidence in decision-making, the love I found in women, and my living out loud. However, at that time, it didn't come, and that acceptance washed over me like the waves of the Caribbean Sea.

Before I left for Aruba, a few friends made plans to come visit me. From old college buddies, my favorite high school teacher, to my best friends, my tribe was coming to check in on me and celebrate this experience. But before they came, I wanted to spend at least a month and a half alone. That alone time was important for me to settle into my body and take in my experience. It was good for me, truly perfection. I took my time to explore the island, find my favorite beach and favorite restaurants, and develop friendships with the new people I met.

I came into a new understanding of settling. Before, I thought settling meant allowing things to happen to me and not being proactive. I'm a fifth-generation hustler. Things didn't happen to me. I happen to them. But this kind of settling allowed me to just be and let the world happen for me and seek God's hand in it all. This settling allowed me to see family beyond my bloodline and take on this concept of tribe. This settling allowed me to embrace the people who were already there. I just had to slow down to see them and let them get near me.

The people in my tribe have different lived experiences and come from all walks of life, but we have shared values that connect us at our core. We love living life. When they came to visit, they each left me a lesson that carried me to the next leg of my journey. Through them, they reminded me I was worthy of having people prioritize caring for me and coming to see about me. Their presence held up a mirror for me and revealed that I was uncomfortable with this attention, even though I knew I needed and craved it. I had to be vulnerable and accept their offering of love and nurturing. This lesson said it was okay for others to have concern for me. I learned to sit in this worthiness. Up to that point, I worked for acceptance and was always *doing* to get it. Instead, I learned I could focus on being who God made me to be, and the healing, the love, the acceptance would appear right before me. Even though my trauma response was to run away, their presence reminded me that I always had someone to run to, that there was always someone whose embrace was waiting for me. And with each goodbye, they tattooed a lesson on my heart as their time with me came to an end.

As my days in Paradise dwindled and I packed my bags to head home, I wasn't sure what I was going home to or what was going to be my physical home. I was in the middle of a real estate transaction that I had invested so much time and money into, and it wasn't looking favorable for me. I wasn't sure what my relationships with my family looked like, and it made me very anxious that moving back home with my mommy may be a reality for me. In hindsight, because I believe in spiritual energy, a major source of anxiety was a premonition about what would befall me the next day, as I would be unjustly detained and jailed.

I didn't know the lessons my tribe left me with gave me the confidence to stay focused and sane during one of my life's horrifying and difficult moments. Their love and support strengthened me, and I felt it most during those lonely moments in my jail cell. The time they spent with me taught me that I wasn't alone, and I could reach out to them in moments of crisis, celebration, and everything in between.

Through my tribe, God showed me He is alive and with me every step of the way. I see God in everything because the people in my tribe reflect His deep love for me. They light my path that gives me the courage to forge forward each day, being proud of the life I live and the choices that make me happy.

MY SAFE WORD

What's your safe word?

If you're into the kinky life, you may use your safe word during your sexual escapades to let your partner(s) know that you need a reprieve. This safe word is an opportunity to step back into reality when you feel that existing circumstances are increasingly overwhelming and you have to tap out, completely or momentarily. In using the safe word, the user reminds themselves they have agency and an inclination to feel safer to stop the action. But I've found safe words can exist outside the bedroom or wherever your pleasure takes you. Safe words alert you, and all parties involved that you no longer feel comfortable, you're going further than you need to, and you need to pull back.

My safe word is sunshine.

I love the sun. Even though I was born during autumn, the sun plays such a big role in my mood and general outlook on life. Many of us in the northern hemisphere experience seasonal affective disorder (SAD). I first learned of this term during my junior year of college. Growing up in the Midwest, I somehow weathered many bone-shaking winters and 4:30 p.m. sunsets. But it wasn't until the stresses of life crept up and laid heavy on me like the mounds of snow that blanketed Chicago during the 2011 Snowmageddon that I was drawn to the campus' counseling and psychological services (CAPS).

I spoke with the counselor on staff, and all I could share was that I wasn't feeling well. At the time, I didn't have the language to determine that I was, in fact, depressed. But I learned a new term, "seasonal affective disorder." According to the Cleveland Clinic, SAD is more than the winter blues. It sets in during the fall and sets in like depression, affecting your everyday life, your mood, and the thoughts that take up space in your mind. I also discovered I suffered from general depression even during the warmest summer months.

The counselor told me there were sunlight therapy lamps I could use when needed. Up to that point, I hadn't realized how important the sun was to me. It was something I assumed would always be there, and I didn't understand its impact until it was gone. But as the years rolled by and more life happened, I became keener to these changes in my body as the sun's rays waned and the winter set in.

Sunshine.

I realized my safe word was sunshine during my winter away in Aruba. From January to April 2021, I lived in Paradise. Where the sun stays constant at eighty-seven degrees, a soft breeze for comfort, thanks to the Atlantic trade winds, and the sun is always sure to shine, even when it rains. At the time, I was moving through some cataclysmic shifts in my life, yet the reminder that I was living in Paradise, as my skin morphed into rich deep chocolate with every sun kiss, I could settle and remember that despite it all, there was sun to be kissed by, and the Caribbean Sea to be swaddled in, and the reassurance of security and comfort was restored.

I recently purchased my first home near Lake Michigan on Chicago's South Side. What I love most about my home are the south-facing windows. When I became a plant mom, the sales associates at the plant nursery would often ask me, "What direction do your windows face?"

"Uhh," *never eat sour watermelon*, "South! They face south." I never knew how important it was or the difference it made until I moved here. From dawn to dusk, the front of my home is the sun's stage. And from my ever-growing fiddle fig leaf tree to my delicate orchids, they get to indulge in one of the greatest gifts offered to us inhabitants of the third planet in the solar system: the sun.

The window ledge is where I rest my lotus-shaped mirror bowl that holds my pyrite, malachite, kyanite, and lapis lazuli crystals. The proximity to the sun's rays and the moon's waves constantly charge my crystals with the intention of igniting a deep fire in me, alchemizing negative energy into healing, giving me strength and confidence to use my voice, realize vision, and gain clarity. With these windows, it seems the sun is able to get to me on the days I need it the most.

These are the days I sink deeper into the dark recesses of my mind and begin to believe the stories I've created based on fear and lack of control of an unknown future. The sun shines on the truth of the reality around me. I am safe and living the blessings I prayed and diligently worked to make space for.

Sunshine.

A simple utterance to remind myself I can take a step out of my thoughts and back into the present moment. The course of thought grounds me in safety, so I can discern reality from the mole hole I'm excavating. It's an opportunity to grab hold of my flotation device and swim back to shore.

Sunshine.

The perfect clear white light that warms my cheek reminds me of the breath in my lungs and the vigorous beat in my chest, maintaining a steady rhythm on my life's journey.

Sunshine.

Like flowers burdened by thick tree branches, a physiological force compels me to use my strength to bend toward the source.

Sunshine.

A spotlight on my parachute, reminding me of the help that comes from the hills.

ACKNOWLEDGMENTS

To my dearest Nicole, the little girl inside. You are such a rockstar, and it's been a pleasure to get to know you. I thank you for your resilience and your discipline to get us where we are today. You, we've, been through a lot, but as our good friend Alex said, "You don't look like what you've been through." God has kept His unfailing hand upon us, and we have graciously and sometimes unknowingly received and relished in that provision. The life you've lived has set us up for the world ahead. We know how to thrive, we know how to make things work, and we know how to show up. Now we can take off that hard armor and rest into *being*. It is here, in this rest, that we can live in our fullest expression. I love you.

To my mommy, my bestie. I love you. I thank you for all you did, doing the best you could at every moment. I thank you for the lessons you've imparted and for being you. For without you, there would be no me. I am glad our love for one another is deep enough to navigate storms. This love allows us to retreat, grow, and reconnect as more whole versions of ourselves. It holds no records of wrongs and is the balm to the wounds we carry.

My dearest beloved, my future wife, my best friend, Tanesha Rae Peeples. I thank God you came into my life when you did. You came at a point when I didn't know where I was going, but I knew I wasn't going back. As I started this new life of being someone who listened to herself and followed her heart, learned to trust herself more than anyone else, and dealt with the resistance to the change, you were there to hold my hand throughout the process. Watched every tear fall and wiped them away. You offered a nonjudgmental loving heart that made it safe to unravel, and you witnessed me put my life back together. Thank you for being the first person to call me a writer. I felt unworthy and out of place when you made that declaration. But it gave me the confidence to own and walk in that part of me. Thank you for believing in me.

To my sister, my first friend. I love you. You encouraged me to write this book but make it more than what happened to me in Aruba. You reminded me that I am more than my lowest and darkest moment.

Thank you to the late Mr. Michael Johnson, my World Literature high school teacher. You taught me the difference between fewer and less and introduced me to great creatives such as August Wilson, William Shakespeare, and Fyodor Dostoevsky. You sparked a thirst to explore more of the written word. I miss you so much; I would have given you a kidney had I known. I know I'm making you proud.

LEKI! My time in AP Composition refined my skills and told me that this writing thing is something I could be good at. You showed me the full breadth of the pen and how we can create a new world with it.

My tribe that traveled over the Caribbean Sea to see about me! LeeAndra Diane, Tamara Drake, Brianna Taylor Jones, Ashley Conorqui, Ebony Dawn Lucas, Dominique Jordan Turner, Kennedy Jordan Turner, Dina Everage, Jasmine Bankhead, Kimberly Waters, Nikita Williamson, Halimah Ibrahim. I love you all!

My author community. Thank you for making this project come to life. Every reader is holding this book in their hands because you chose to make my vision a reality. You were the FIRST to purchase my breakout BOOK! You all are my DAY ONES! I cannot thank you enough: Tracy Roeback, Jeffery Beckham, Latrice Eggleston Williams, Jalynn M. Lassic, Kimberly Marie McJunkins, John Sciberras, Ashley Willis, LaKia Wright, Andrea Bell, Alexandria Willis, Tamara L Hoff, Sarah Clapper, Amy Galibois, Elena Martin, Tanesha Peeples, Nameka Bates, Denetrice Hale, Sasha Pena, Harold M. Moore, Aya-Nikole Cook, Ella McCann, Rachael Carbone, Cat Jonassen, Brianna Jones, Kaila Turner, Patricia Brumley, Bry Delicia, Rha-Kera Sutton, Oren Jacobson, Melody Waller, LaTonya Saqiid, Marsha Washington, Robert Smith III, Michelle Rashad and Imagine Englewood If, Imani Maatuka, Noelle Elizabeth Sanford, Quentin J. Scott, Ariel Joy Thomas, Alescia Farr, Amanda Dunlap, Eileen Dordek, Valentine Dike Jr., Amber Townsend, Shanelle Covington, Kimberly Cummins, Ronda Hale Johnson, Dan Johnson, Toi Logan, Shayla Bell, Aditi Singh, Kayin Barclay, Rosemarin King, LeeAndra Khan, Latoya Buchanan, Alicia Rankin, Nakia Hunter, Ebony Dawn Lucas, Lenita Gipson, Natalie Richards, Cabrina Bundy, Vashti Hale, Karyn Smith, Julia Dennis, Ashley Conorqui, Josie Morris, Eric Koester, Brooke McKean, Jamese Dunlap, Allie Verbeke, Michael Davis, Jamila Mattox,

Dani Jackson, Sheila R. Bew, Tosha Downey, Jaylin McClinton, Noufo Nabine, Riley Jones, Danielle Berry, Darnisha Holliday, Jaidah Turnbow, Dominique Jordan Turner, Robbie Curry, Derrick Fleming Jr., Skyler Larrimore, Monica Swope, Jameika Sampson, Kimi Ellen, Skye Frank, Jamil Simmons, Gabriela Garcia, Marcus Gill, Rita G. Lewis, Joann Dixon, Tara McDonald, LaShawn Holloway, Dori Collins, Ty Nicole Tucker, Christian Johns, Shavon Banket, Gabrielle Herndon, Ti'Kyra Napoleon, Liza Booker, Love Morgan, Gizelle Clemens, Ebonee Dawson, Rebekah Sharpe, Aaja Magee, Donald Grayson, Ekua McGinnis, Nichole Hurst, Kamaria Morris, Akilah Bradford, Danielle McConnell, Jakendra Williams, Trevor Wilkins, Ashley Williams, Avanii Hazzard, Eva Robinson, Tamiya Goggins, Tanikia Carpenter, Cherice L. Price, JeNai Talley Jackson, Lauren Underwood, Wendy R. McCulley, and Tosin Shenbanjo.

I thank God for making me, blessing me with these gifts to share my story, the courage to look it squarely in the eyes and put it on paper, and the voice to amplify it.

APPENDIX

HOMECOMING: RETURN TO SELF AND COUNTRY
The Holy Bible. Johnson 10:10, World English Version.
The Holy Bible. Matthew 10:19–20, World English Version.

THE SANCTITY OF LIFE
The Holy Bible. John 10:10, World English Version.

BUT, I BELIEVE ME
Gregory, James N.. "1. The Second Great Migration: A Historical Overview" In *African American Urban History since World War II* edited by Kenneth L. Kusmer and Joe W. Trotter, 19–38. Chicago: University of Chicago Press, 2009. https://doi.org/10.7208/9780226465128-004

Jeffries, John. *Wartime American: The World War II Home Front.* Chicago: Ivan R. Dee, 2012.

Stixx, Nikki. "Hustle." Urban Dictionary, February 24, 2019. https://www.urbandictionary.com/define.php?term=hustle.

MY LAST SUMMER IN THE HOOD

Demby, Gene. "Making the Case That Discrimination is Bad for Your Health." NPR, January 14, 2018. https://www.npr.org/sections/codeswitch/2018/01/14/577664626/making-the-case-that-discrimination-is-bad-for-your-health.

Knowles-Carter, Beyonce. Bigger. Parkwood Entertainment. July 1, 2019.

Pierce, Joe. "Derrick Rose Says He 'Kind of Got PTSD' While Growing Up in Chicago." *Complex,* February 14, 2020. https://www.complex.com/sports/2020/02/derrick-rose-ptsd-mental-health-chicago-childhood.

Recktenwald, William. "Police Sweep Targets Crack Link Between Suburbs and South Side." *Chicago Tribune,* July 09, 1992. https://www.chicagotribune.com/news/ct-xpm-1992-07-09-9203020089-story.html.

Te, Ashley. "Social Infrastructure is Key: Chicago's Deadly 1995 Heatwave." *History of Yesterday,* June 2, 2021. https://historyofyesterday.com/social-infrastructure-chicagos-deadly-1995-heatwave-8c072b67c50c.

Terry, Don. "In a Chicago Neighborhood Overrun with Crime, a Serial Killer Almost Walks Away." *New York Times,* June 26, 1995. https://www.nytimes.com/1995/06/26/us/in-a-chicago-neighborhood-overrun-with-crime-a-serial-killer-almost-walks-away.html.

MAMA GOTTA HAVE A LIFE, TOO

Katie, Byron. *Loving What Is: Four Questions That Can Change Your Life.* New York City: Penguin Random House, LLC., 2002.

GOD IS LOVE IS LOVE

Lorde, Audre. Scratching the Surface: Some Notes on Barriers to Women and Loving. The Black Scholar, 9:7,31–35, DOI: 10.1080/00064246.1978.11414006.

TRIBE

Doby, Danielle. *I Am Her Tribe*. Kansas City, MO: Andrews McMeel Publishing, 2018.

MY SAFE WORD

Cleveland Clinic. "Seasonal Depression (Seasonal Affective Disorder)." 2022. https://my.clevelandclinic.org/health/diseases/9293-seasonal-depression.

Made in the USA
Middletown, DE
24 September 2022